UNLOCKING THE PAST

WHAT STORIES DOES YOUR SCHOOL HAVE TO REVEAL?

A COMPENDIUM TO *'A SECONDARY EDUCATION FOR ALL'*?

UNLOCKING THE PAST

WHAT STORIES DOES YOUR SCHOOL HAVE TO REVEAL?

A COMPENDIUM TO *'A SECONDARY EDUCATION FOR ALL'?*

JOHN ANDREWS & DEBORAH TOWNS

Australian Scholarly

The History Council of Victoria Inc. commissioned the authors of this book to write a centenary history of post-primary education in Victoria and provided support to Australian Scholarly for its publication.

Published 2017 by
Australian Scholarly Publishing Pty Ltd
7 Lt Lothian St Nth, North Melbourne, Vic 3051
Tel: 03 9329 6963 / Fax: 03 9329 5452
enquiry@scholarly.info / www.scholarly.info

ISBN 978-1-925588-50-7

Cover design Wayne Saunders

Contents

Your School's History – At a Glance

School identity is an important part of school life. Communities everywhere are proud of their local school, what it has achieved for past and present students, how it has cared for and nurtured them and the values and programs it has provided over time. Such values and attitudes help ensure that all students, parents and teachers have that sense of belonging. Rediscovering and celebrating that identity is important to many students who attended government secondary schools and to their families. It can be expressed through the histories people have written about their school. But to acquire that identity and history it is essential that historians and school community members unlock the records – including oral history sources – to reveal the rich, enlightening and sometimes amusing history of the local school. Government secondary education in Victoria is, at the time of print, 112 years old, the first government school, the Melbourne Continuation School opening in 1905. From humble but hopeful beginnings government secondary education has responded to the needs of communities and the state. It has become a rich, varied and complex heritage and has supplied vital human resources contributing to all areas of endeavour for the nation's benefit. That history needs to be discovered, captured, retold and built upon as the decades pass. And equally, every effort needs to be made to guarantee the survival of those histories of individual schools that together make up the educational history of the state and its citizens.

Sources for Your School History

Official documents such as gazettes, education newspapers, annual reports, parliamentary papers, magazines and government files (including closed schools) held in the Public Records Office of Victoria, and the State Library of Victoria as well as in local repositories have been a rich resource of information as we researched *'A secondary education for all'?*. They will be for schools who want to write and enrich their histories. These resources need to be tapped because they reveal parts of the multi-faceted experience and political and educational environment that influences the history of every school. That story is fleshed out and enriched by an increasing number of school histories and school magazines that have emerged over time. They have become an increasingly important resource as schools and individual past students seek to find out more about their school days and how their school has grown and met challenges over those years. They tell us about sporting and cultural achievements, of individual student and teacher contributions and awards and of the myriad of activities that contribute to the academic, sporting, cultural and social life of schools.

Photographs such as those that appear in newsletters, on websites, and in magazines including those that record each class every year add information about well-known students and teachers, changing trends in school uniforms and any changes in school names. Add to these collections of photographs taken for department annual reports, curriculum publications and the ever changing collection of education newspapers and magazines that have emerged in recent decades as well as collections created by teacher unions, principals' associations, subject associations and other interested bodies and the resource becomes an inestimable collection for posterity. The value of visual sources is acknowledged at every school reunion when students past and present are asked to contribute their own photographs to reunion displays and may be invited to suggest missing names in class photos. Programs for school plays, concerts, musicals and speech nights contribute further, indicating trends and fashions in school life and in the wider community generally. And then there are the contributions of respective governments and the hordes of volunteers through mothers' clubs, parents' clubs, school committees, school councils, working bees and classroom support who keep the school going and focussed. Volunteers save millions of taxpayer dollars every year for their school. Their histories too need to be told and included in every school history. They will celebrate achievements in providing improved facilities such as school halls and gymnasiums and the frustrating campaigns that often preceded the acquisition of new buildings, facilities and funded new programs. Recognition also needs to be made about the contributions of students through war savings funds, social service clubs, appeals and monetary and in-kind contributions as part of student leadership, government and active citizenship initiatives that have affected lives within local communities, the state, nation and indeed globally. The changes and continuities of schools and societies are reflected through all of these activities and the documents that record them across the decades.

Local libraries and historical societies as well as local and regional newspapers likewise embellish the stories that emanate from schools. In some instances new stories as well as missing details can enrich and flesh out your school's history, even treading into unknown territories. In some instances where there was controversy, divisions within a community or just differences of opinion, historical societies and local newspapers may have recorded the details that are missing in official documents. The names of buildings such as halls, libraries, sporting complexes and indeed in some instances, the name of the school itself reveal the names of local identities, achievers or important people associated with the local area. Such stories make the history more enjoyable and rewarding for the reader.

That school history is becoming increasingly important is reflected in the fact that many schools now have an archivist to ensure that records are saved, organised into orderly and easily-navigated files and made available to all with an interest in their school, family or personal history. Many schools have already written histories or part of it, often in connection with a recent or distant milestone. We have recorded these in the section below, Does your school have a history? – Print and web histories, beginning at page 71. Some schools such as Frankston High School and Melbourne Boys' High School have, for some years, maintained and expanded a museum, Frankston's being established in 2015. The school's history is told using the types of resources identified here. As well visitors will find honour boards and school uniforms to help complete the picture. Open to the public, the museum is also used as a teaching resource for school and local history. School history is indeed a heritage that should be encouraged, nurtured and supported.

Print documents often record the positive sides of a school's history, often leaving out the details about arguments, heated debates, conflict and the 'juicy bits' of every story. Oral history can be immeasurably value in filling in the gaps and bringing your school's history to life. Even stories about getting to school, the mishaps of the school bus, of friendships made and sustained over the years. Every school has had its colourful characters amongst its students, parents and teachers. Interviews with past and present students help to bring such stories and anecdotes to life as well as help to fill those historical gaps.

Using the Abbreviated Histories

Many schools have changed their status and names over time. Some name changes may be quite recent and yet the school may have a far longer history. Schools have been listed in this compendium using their current or, if now closed, their most recent name. The second column traces the major changes in status and name of each school from its beginnings to its current or most recent identity. The information contained about your school in the rather lengthy table that follows is only the start of recording every school's history – but it is an important and crucial starting point.

The authors have made every effort to be accurate and comprehensive. If you are able to correct any inaccuracies that may have been included or provide any missing details (indicated by a question mark), please contact the authors at acesja@gmail.com. Some school changes and mergers, as the table below shows, have been quite complex and it is becoming increasingly important to record those changes while those who still remember these changes are able to provide missing details. Some secondary schools began as primary (national, elementary or state) schools and later became post-primary schools, or, as enrolments dropped, some merged their primary and post-primary schools or reverted to being primary schools only. Such details need to be identified, and where necessary, unravelled and recorded for the future. More schools today combine primary and secondary classes, sharing teachers, resources and expertise for the benefit of all students.

The following abbreviations have been used to denote school types. Such a list together with the fact that many schools are now called Colleges, is further evidence that different times and different student cohorts have needed to be catered for in different ways over time. They reflect the collective educational wisdom (or lack of it) from time to time.

List of Abbreviations

AHS	Agricultural High School
BHS	Boys' High School
CS	Central School/Classes
Cont	Continuation School
Cos	Consolidated School
DAS	Domestic Arts School
GHS	Girls' High School
GSS	Girls' Secondary School
GTS	Girls Technical School
GS	Group School
HES	Higher Elementary School
HS	High School
JTS	Junior Technical School
P-10 (12)	Prep-Year 10 (12) College
PPS	Post Primary School
PS	Primary School
SC	Secondary College
SDS	Special Development School
SpS	Special School
SS	State School
STS	Senior Technical School
TS	Technical School
THS	Technical High School

School	History
Albert Park College	1. South Melbourne HS – 1918; Renamed Albert Park HS – 1968 2. South Melbourne TS – 1919 (1988–2001 Correspondence School) 1 and 2 merged as Hobson's Bay SC – 1988; Closed – 2006; Reopened as Albert Park College – 2011
Alexandra SC	HES – 1937; HS – 1953; SC – 1990
Alkira SC, Cranbourne North	Casey Central SC – 2009; Renamed Alkira SC – 2010
Allambie Centre	Presbyterian Neglected Children's Society School opened at North Melbourne (Errol Street) SS – 1907; Became independent of the school – 1923; Moved to Burwood and renamed Kildonan Presbyterian Children's Home – 1938; Became a government school and renamed Allambie – 1961; Closed – 1990
Alpine School for Student Leadership	Alpine School (Dinner Plains) – 1999; Snowy River Campus, Marlo – 2007; Gnurad-Gundidj Campus, Mount Noorat – 2009
Altona North TS	1959; Closed – 1992
Altona P-9 College	Altona HS – 1959; SC – 1993; Merged with Altona West PS – 2010
Alvie CoS	SS – 1890; CoS – 1952; CoSPS – 1966; CS – 1991

Apollo Bay P-12 College	Middleton SS – 1875; Renamed Krambrook SS – 1879; Renamed Apollo Bay SS – c.1908; GS – 1952; CoS – 1953; HES – 1977; P-12 – 1991
Ararat College	1. HES – 1912; HS – 1913 2. Ararat TS – 1969 1 and 2 merged as Ararat SC – 1990; Renamed Ararat Community College – 1997; Ararat College – 2009
Ascot Vale SpS	1980
Ashwood College	1. Jordanville TS – 1954 2. Ashwood HS – 1958 1 and 2 merged as Ashwood SC – 1988
Ashwood School	Ashwood SpS – 1976; Renamed Ashwood School – 1989
Aspendale TS	TS – 1959; Closed – 1992
Auburn CS	Opened as Red Gum Flat SS – 1889; CS – ?; PS – ?
Austin Hospital School, Heidelberg	1902; First Department teacher appointed – 1908; Closed – 1932; Reopened – 1940
Avenues Education, Moorabbin	1. Alfred Hospital SpS – 1955; Closed – 1981 2. South East Child and Family Education Centre – 1981; Renamed Alfred Education Centre – 1996; Renamed Avenues Education – 2009
Avoca CS	SS – 1878; CS – 1924; PS – 1928
Avondale SC	Avondale Heights HS – 1972; Avondale SC – 1989; Closed – 1991

Bacchus Marsh College	HS – 1921; HES – 1931; HS – 1951; SC – 1990; College – 2001
Baden Powell P-9 College, Tarneit	2008
Baimbridge College	1. Hamilton HES – 1912; Hamilton and District HS – 1915; Hamilton HS – 1916 2. Hamilton TS – 1961; SC – 1990 1 and 2 merged as Baimbridge College – 1992; P-12 – 2003
Bairnsdale SC	1. HS – 1912 2. North Gippsland School of Mines – 1889; Bairnsdale JTS – 1915; TS – 1941 1 and 2 merged as SC – 1992
Ballarat HS	AHS and Cont – 1907; HS – 1917
Ballarat Hospital After Care SpS	1946; Closed – 1952
Ballarat SC	1. Ballarat East HS – 1955; SC – 1991 2. Ballarat North JTS – 1955; TS – 1959; Renamed Midlands SC – 1990 3. Wendouree HTS – 1978; SC – 1990 1, 2, and 3 merged as Ballarat SC – 1994
Ballarat School of Mines	1870; JTS – 1913; Girls TS – 1959; Ballarat TS – 1968; Closed – 1977
Ballarat Specialist School	Ballarat SDS – 1955; Ballarat SpS – 1963

Ballarat (Urquhart Street) PS	SS – 1878; CS – 1939; PS – 1951; Relocated and renamed Urquhart Park PS – 1982
Ballerrt Murrup College – A Koorie Pathways School, Glenroy	KODE Campus, Box Forest SC – 1995; Renamed Victorian P-12 College of Koorie Education – 2006; Renamed Ballert Murrup – 2009; Closed – 2012
Balmoral K-12 Community College	1. Common School – 1859; PS – 1867; GS – 1950; CoS – 1955 HS – 1968 2. Balmoral & 3. District Kindergarten 1 and 2 merged as Balmoral P-12 Community College – 2009; Renamed as K-12 – 2011, incorporating 3.
Baltara School, Thomastown	1. Parkville – Royal Park SpS – 1943; Renamed Turana SpS – 1954; Baltara SpS and Reception Centre – 1968–92; Renamed Parkville Youth Reception Centre – 1992; Closed – 2012 2. Ascot Vale Secure Welfare campus – 1995 3. Maribyrnong Secure Welfare campus – 1992 4. Thomastown – Baltara Integration Unit – 1995; Renamed Thomastown Integration Unit – 2008 All renamed Baltara School – 2004 5. Hurstbridge Farm – 2008 6. Preston Integration Unit – Opened at Heidelberg Heights PS – ?; Relocated to and renamed as Olympic Village Social Integration Unit – ?; Merged with Baltara School – 2011; Renamed Preston Integration Unit – 2012
Balwyn HS	1954

Bamawm CS	1912; Closed – 1954
Baringa SpS, Moe	Moe Special School – 1974; Renamed Baringa Special School – 1981
Barwon Valley School, Belmont	1. Presbyterian Church Hall Spastic Centre – 1949; Geelong Hospital Spastic School – 1954; Closed – 1962 2. Karingal Day Training Centre – 1952; Karingal SDS – ? 3. Corilong Day Training Centre – 1963; Became a government school, Corio SDS – 1989 2 and 3 merged as Barwon Valley SDS – 1992 4. Shannon Park SpS – ?; Joined Barwon Valley School – 1993
Bass Coast Specialist School, Wonthaggi	2009
Bayside P-12 College	1. Altona North HS – 1960 2. Paisley HS – 1972; SC – 1991 3. Williamstown TS – 1954; Renamed Williamstown North SC – 1990 1, 2 and 3 merged as Bayside SC – 1993; P-12 College – 2007
Bayside SDS Moorabbin	Moorabbin SDS – 1986; Bayside SDS – 1987
Bayswater SC	HS – 1961; SC – 1991
Beaufort SC	SS – 1864; HES – 1925; HS – 1960; SC – 1990

Beechworth SC	HES – 1912; HS – 1959; SC – 1990
Beechworth Training Prison School	1955; Closed – 2004
Bellarine SC, Drysdale	Queenscliff HES – 1945; HS – 1957; Renamed Bellarine SC – 1996
Belmont HS	HS – 1955
Belmore School, Balwyn	Yooralla Hospital School for Crippled Children – Balwyn Annex – 1962; Belmore School – 1989
Belvoir – Wodonga SpS, Wodonga	Murray Valley Day Training Centre – 1983; Belvoir SpS – 1984; Belvoir-Wodonga SDS – 1996
Benalla College	1. HES – 1912; HS – 1915 2. TS – 1963 1 and 2 merged as SC – 1990; College – 1994
Bendigo Base Hospital School	1950–1951
Bendigo JTS	JTS – 1909–62
Bendigo School for Deaf Children Bendigo Deaf facility	Became a government school – 1953; Closed – 1963; Reopened – 1964; Bendigo Deaf Facility – ?
Bendigo Senior SC	Cont – 1907; HS – 1912; Senior HS – 1976; Senior SC – 1989

Bendigo South East College	1. Bendigo DAS – 1916; GSS – 1935; GHS – 1966; Renamed Flora Hill HS – 1974; SC – 1990 2. Golden Square HS – 1960; 7–10 School – 1978; SC – 1990 1 and 2 merged as Bendigo South East College – 2008
Bendigo SDS	Peter Harcourt Day Training Centre for the Mentally Retarded – 1966; Bendigo SDS – 1991
Bendigo Training Prison	1955; Closed – 2006
Bentleigh SC	1. Bentleigh HS – 1956 2. Moorabbin TS – 1954 1 and 2 merged as Moorabbin City THS – 1984; Renamed Moorabbin City SC – 1988; Renamed Bentleigh SC – 1997
Berendale School, Hampton East	Moorabbin West SpS – 1965; Renamed Berendale – 1987
Berwick SC	HS – 1977; SC – 1991
Beulah CS	Coliban Upper SS – 1909; Renamed Beulah CS – 1910; Renamed Beulah East SS – 1929; Closed – 1954
Birchip P-12 School	HES – 1922; HS – 1964; Birchip Community Education Complex – 1980; P-12 School – 1995
Blackburn CS	1953; Closed – 1955

Blackburn English Language School	Eastbridge Language Centre; Renamed Blackburn South Language Centre – ?; Renamed Blackburn English Language School – 1989
Blackburn HS	1956
Blackburn SC	TS – 1959; SC – 1991; Closed – 1992
Blackburn South HS	HS – 1959; Closed – 1989
Blackwood Special Schools Outdoor Education Centre	Church of England Golden Point School No. 269 – 1855; Moved to new site at Red Hill – 1915; Renamed SS 1074 Mt Blackwood – 1918; Renamed Blackwood School No. 1074 – 1928; Closed – 1969; Reopened as the Blackwood School Camp for Intellectually Handicapped Children – 1970; Renamed Blackwood Special Schools Outdoor Education Centre – 1981; Incorporated – 1995
Bogong Outdoor Education Centre	1. Bogong School Camp – 1971; Renamed Bogong Outdoor Education Centre – ? 2. 15 Mile Creek PS merged with the Centre – 2010
Boisdale CoS	CoS – 1953
Bonegilla Migrant Centre School	1952; Closed – 1971
Boort District School	HES opened and closed – 1915; Reopened – 1920; HS – 1963; SC – 1990; Merged with Boort PS – 2009

Boronia K-12 College	1. Boronia TS – 1973; Boronia Heights SC – 1990; Renamed Boronia Heights College – 2002 2. Allandale Kindergarten; PS – 1923 1 and 2 merged as Boronia K-12 College in 2012
Box Hill HS	1930
Box Hill Senior SC	1. Boys JTS – 1943 2. Box Hill Girls' Technical School – 1924; Renamed Whitehorse Technical College –1971 1 and 2 merged and renamed Box Hill TS – 1985 (while the TAFE sector was renamed Whitehorse College of TAFE and merged with the Box Hill College of TAFE as the Box Hill Institute – 1984); Renamed Box Hill Senior SC – 1993; Specialist school in Sporting development – 2009
Brandon Park SC, Mulgrave	TS – 1978; SC – 1989; Closed – 2003
Brauer College, Warrnambool	Warrnambool TS – 1911; Department school – 1945; Renamed Brauer College – 1990
Braybrook College	HS – 1960; SC – 1991; College – 2000
Brentwood SC	HS – 1969; SC – 1991
Bright P-12 College	Morse's Creek Common School – 1865; HES – 1918; Renamed Bright P-12 College – 1991

Brighton SC	1. HS – 1955 2. Boys TS – 1922–88; Cora Lyn DAS – 1924–66 1 and 2 merged as SC – 1989
Brighton Bay SC	TS – 1921; SC –1989; Closed – 1992
Broadford SC	HES – 1960; HS – 1962; SC – 1990
Broadmeadows TS	1961; Closed – 1992
Brookside P-9 College, Caroline Springs	Caroline Springs College – 2000; Brookside P-9 – 2012
Brunswick SC	1. Brunswick TS – 1916 2. Brunswick HS – 1964 3. Brunswick Boys' School – 1888; Brunswick DAS – 1924; GSS – 1935; GHS – 1969; Brunswick East HS – 1983 1, 2 and 3 merged as Brunswick SC – 1993
Brunswick West CS Albert Street	CS – 1873; PS – 1970; Closed – 1996
Bruthen CS	SS – 1872; CS – ?; PS – ?
Buckley Park College, Essendon	HS – 1963; SC – 1990; College – 2001
Bulleen Heights School	?

Bundoora SC	Greenwood HS – 1971; SC – 1991; Renamed Bundoora SC – 1996
Burwood East SDS	1. Opened as part of the Alkira Centre, Box Hill – 1954; Renamed Burwood East SDS – 1985 2. Wattle Heights SDS merged with Burwood East – 1996
Burwood HS	HS – 1955; Closed – 1987
Camberwell CS	Common School – 1867; CS – 1926; PS – 1968
Camberwell HS	1941
Camperdown College	HES – 1920; HS – 1945; Merged with PS as P-12 College – 1995
Camp Hill CS, Bendigo	Camp Hill SS – 1878; Bendigo Cont – 1907; CS – 1916; Central Classes discontinued – 1935; Renamed PS – 1951
Cann River P-12 College	Cann River – 1915; Building opened – 1927; SS – 1937; CS – 1965; HES – 1986; P-12 College – 1990
Canterbury Girls SC	East Camberwell GHS – 1928; East Camberwell GSS – 1949; Renamed Camberwell GSS – 1952; Camberwell GHS – 1958; Canterbury GHS – 1961; SC – 1990
Carranballac P-9 College, Point Cook	1. Boardwalk SC – 2002 2. Jamieson Way SC – 2006 1 and 2 merged – 2006

Carronbank School for Partially Sighted Children	1961; Closed – after 1972?
Carrum Downs SC	2004
Carwatha College P-12, Noble Park	Noble Park North HS – 1977; Carwatha HS – 1981; SC – 1990; College P-12 – 2003
Casterton SC	HES – 1914; HS – 1953; SC – 1990
Castlemaine Reformatory School	1924; Closed – 1951
Castlemaine SC	1. HS – 1910 2. School of Mines and Industries – 1887; Renamed Castlemaine TS – 1903; JTS – 1916; T College – 1958 1 and 2 merged as SC – 1994
Caulfield Junior College Balaclava Road	Balaclava SS – 1914; Renamed Caulfield North CS – 1916; Renamed Caulfield Junior College – 1989
Caulfield North CS	Opened as Balaclava SS – 1914; Renamed Caulfield North Central School – 1916; PS – ?; Closed – ?
Caulfield Park Community School	St Kilda Alternative HS – 1975; Renamed Caulfield Park Community School – 1987
Chadstone HS	HS – 1962; Closed – 1989

Chaffey SC, Mildura	Mildura TS – 1955; Chaffey SC – 1990; Years 7–10 – 1996
Charles La Trobe College, Ivanhoe	1. Macleod TS – 1960 2. Rosanna HS – 1958; Renamed La Trobe HS – 1966 3. Heidelberg GSS – 1957; GHS – 1969; Renamed Waterdale HS – 1973; Merged with LaTrobe HS – 1983; Renamed La Trobe SC – 1989 4. Heidelberg HS – 1955 5. Heidelberg TS – 1954 4 and 5 merged as Banksia SC – 1989 6. La Trobe SC and Banksia SC merged as Banksia La Trobe SC – 2008; Renamed Charles La Trobe College – 2010
Charlton College	1. HES – 1912; HS – 1966; SC – 1990 2. North Central Technical Centre – 1978 1 and 2 merged as Charlton SC – 1994 Charlton SC merged with Charlton PS as P-12 College – 1995; Renamed Charlton College – 2009
Cheltenham SC	HS – 1959; SC – 1988
Children's Cottages, Kew	1929; Closed – 2001
Children's Hospital School, Mount Macedon	1942; Closed – 1943
Chiltern CS	SS – 1874; CS – 1912; PS – mid-1950s?
Clayton TS	1961; Closed – 1992

Clunes HES	SS – 1875; North and South Clunes SS amalgamated as Clunes SS – 1892; HES – 1912; PS – 1955
Cobden TS	1969
Cobram PS	SS – 1888; CoS – 1952; PS – 1962
Cobram SC	HS – 1962; SC – 1989
Cobram and District SpS	Cobram Day Training Centre – 1972; Became a government school and renamed Cobram SDS – 1976; Renamed Cobram Special School – ?
Coburg PS (HES)	Pentridge National School – 1853; Pentridge Common School – 1862; Renamed Coburg Common School – 1870; Coburg SS – 1872; Coburg HES – 1911; Coburg PS – 1912
Coburg Senior HS	1. HS – 1916 2. Preston HS – 1964; SC – 1994 1 and 2 merged as Coburg-Preston SC – 1996; Merged with Coburg East PS and renamed Coburg P-12 College on former RMIT Campus – 1996; Renamed Moreland SC and East Coburg PS closed – 1997; Closed – 2004; Reopened as Coburg Senior HS – 2007
Coburg SDS	Coburg Day Training Centre – 1984; Department school and named Coburg SDS – 1989
Cohuna Consolidated	HES – 1924; CoS – 1948
Cohuna SC	HS – 1955; SC – 1991

Colac SC	1. AHS – 1911; HS – 1918 2. TS – 1961; Renamed Colac College – 1997; Renamed Colac SC – 2008
Colac SpS	Colanda Education Unit – 1985; Became a government school, Colac SDS – 1986; Colac SpS – 1998
Coleraine CS	Coleraine SS – 1878; CS – 1918; PS – 1958
Collingwood CS, Cambridge Street	SS – 1877; CS – 1922; PS – 1933; Closed – 1992
Collingwood College	DAS – 1915; GHS – 1936; HS – 1968; Merged with Cromwell Street SS (1912) as Education Centre (P-12) – 1975; Renamed Collingwood College – 1990
Collingwood English Language School	1. Victoria Park English Language Centre – 1981 2. Collingwood Language School – 1981 1 and 2 merged as the Collingwood English Language Centre – 1989
Collingwood Home of Hope Orphanage School	Collingwood Home of Hope Orphanage School – 1916; Closed – 1925
Collingwood TS	STS – 1912; JTS added – 1913; Closed – 1987
Concord School, Bundoora	Watsonia SpS – 1973; Renamed Concord School – 1988

Copperfield College, Delahey	Kings Park HS – 1979; Renamed Kings Park SC with new Delahey campus – 1993; Renamed Copperfield College with Sydenham campus opening – 1998
Corryong College	1. Rural School, Corryong – 1972; Renamed SS – 1874; Renamed Corryong Upper Murray HS – 1877; HES – 1917; CoS – 1951 2. HS – 1952; SC – 1990 1 and 2 merged as P-12 College – 2002
Cowes CS	?
Craigieburn SC	PPS – 1984; SC – 1990
Cranbourne East SC	2011
Cranbourne SC	HS – 1976; SC – 1990
Creekside K-9 College, Caroline Springs	Caroline Springs College – 2000; Creekside – 2012
Croxton SpS	1957; Renamed Croxton School – 1995
Croydon Community School	Mitcham HS Extension – 1974; Croydon Community – 1981
Croydon SDS	Monkaymi Day Training Centre – 1978; Croydon SDS – 1990
Crusoe 7–10 SC, Kangaroo Flat	Kangaroo Flat TS – 1962; SC – 1990; Renamed Bendigo South West SC – 2008; Renamed Crusoe 7–10 – 2009

Dalton's Bridge	Opened as Gunbower Island CS – 1923; Renamed Dalton's Bridge Central – c.1925; Closed – 1948
Dandenong HS	1. HS – 1919 2. Dandenong GSS – 1957; GHS – 1966; Renamed Dandenong North HS – 1973; Renamed Cleeland HS – 1974; SC – 1991 3. Doveton TS – 1963; SC – 1991 1, 2 and 3 merged as the new Dandenong HS – 2007
Dandenong Valley SC	JTS – 1954; SC – 1990; Closed – 1991
Dandenong Valley SDS	Wallara Care Centre – 1959; Wallara Day Centre – 1961; Dandenong Valley SDS (Government school) – 1983; Dandenong Valley School – 1989; Reverted to Dandenong Valley SDS – 2011
Daylesford SC	1. Daylesford School of Mines – 1890; TS – 1914; THS – 1946; SC – 1991 2. HES – 1912; Merged with TS – 1943
Dean HES	1911 (Victoria's first); Central classes – 1916; Discontinued – 1934
Derrinallum P-12 College	HES – 1959; HS – 1963; SC – 1990; P-12 Merged with PS – 1994
Diamond Valley College	1. Hurstbridge HS – 1966 2. Diamond Creek TS – 1973 1 and 2 merged as Diamond Valley College – 1988

Diamond Valley SDS	Opened as Ivanhoe Helping Hand Day Training Centre – 1939; Senior section renamed Ivanhoe/ Diamond Valley Activity Therapy Centre – 1977; Junior section renamed Heidelberg SDS – 1977; New school renamed Diamond Valley SDS – 1987
Dimboola Memorial SC	Dimboola HES – 1921; HS – 1945; Renamed Dimboola Memorial HS – 1947; SC – 1987
Dingee CoS	SS – 1889; CoS – 1947; Closed – 1982
Distance Education Centre Victoria (DECV)	Correspondence School (Secondary) – 1922; DECV – 1993
Donald PS	SS – 1873; HES – 1912; PS – 1960
Donald HS	HS – 1961
Doncaster SC	HS – 1969; SC – 1991
Dromana SC	TS – 1967; SC – 1989
Drouin SC	Central Classes – 1953; HS – 1956; SC – 1990
Dumbalk CS	1890; Closed – 1891
SS183 Dunkeld CoS	Dunkeld National School – 1855; PS – 1884; GS – 1952–53; CoS – 1954
Eaglehawk CS	National School – 1854; SS – 1874; CS – 1920; PS – 1964
Eaglehawk SC	HS – 1964; THS – 1978; SC – 1991
East Doncaster SC	Doncaster East HS – 1974; SC – 1994

East Gippsland Specialist School, Bairnsdale	2004
East Loddon P-12 College	Loddon East SS – 1951; GS – 1953; East Loddon Cons – 1954; HS – 1973; Renamed P-12 – 1990; Renamed Eastern Ranges School – 2012
East Oakleigh CS	1936; Closed – 1955
Eastern Ranges School	Voluntary group in Canterbury – ?; Named Irabina SDS – 1991; Renamed Wantirna Heights School – ?; Renamed Eastern Ranges School – 2012
Echuca College	1. JTS – 1917; SC – 1989 2. HS – 1912 1 and 2 merged as College – 2006
Echuca Specialist School	Tehan House/Echuca SDS – 1991; Became a government school, Echuca Specialist School – 1997
Edenhope College	HES – 1952; CoS – 1953; HS – 1959; Edenhope SC – 1991; College – 1994
Elisabeth Murdoch College, Langwarrin	Langwarrin PPS – 1984; HS – 1984; SC – 1990; Renamed Elisabeth Murdoch College – 2004
Eltham HS	HES – 1926; HS – 1950
Elwood CS	1917–56
Elwood College	HS – 1957; SC – 1989; College – 1994

Emerald SC	PPS – 1985; SC – 1988
Emerson School, Dandenong	Dandenong Special School – 1973; Emerson – 1984; Second campus (former Lyndale-Greenslopes PS) – 2012
Endeavour Hills SC	Doveton North TS – 1969; Endeavour Hills TS – 1970–73; Endeavour Hill SC – 1990; Eumemmerring SC – 1992; Endeavour Hills SC – 2009
Epping SC	HS – 1976; SC – 1990
Essendon – Keilor College	1. West Melbourne TS – 1912; Renamed Essendon TS – 1938 2. Essendon HES – 1913; HS – 1914 1 and 2 merged as Queens Park SC – 1990 3. Niddrie HS – 1959 4. East Keilor HS – 1968; Keiior Heights SC – 1990; College – 1990 Queens Park SC 3 and 4 merged as Essendon – East Keilor District College – 1993
Euroa SC	1. HES – 1919; HS – 1956 2. Euroa TS – ? 1 and 2 merged as SC – 1992
Ewing House School for Deaf Children, Ballarat	Victorian Committee for the Promotion of Oral Education for the Deaf – 1950; Ewing House School – 1952; Closed – 2003
Fairfield North CS	PS – 1928; CS – 1952–54; PS – 1955; Closed – 1992

Fairhills HS, Ferntree Gully	1973
Ferntree Gully College	1. JTS – 1954; TS – 1955; Glenfern SC – 1991 2. HS – 1968; SC – 1990 1 and 2 merged as College – 1997; Closed – 2006
Fitzroy HS	1. Fitzroy SS – 1874; DAS – 1911; Girls' School – 1930; GSS – 1950; Renamed Exhibition HS – 1976 2. Fitzroy CS – 1915; HS – 1957 1 and 2 merged as Fitzroy SC – 1988; Closed – 1992; Reopened as Fitzroy HS – 2004
Fitzroy (Bell Street) Special School	SS – 1878; SpS – 1913; Closed – 1979
Flemington SC	GHS – 1949; HS – 1964; SC – 1990; Closed – 1992
Footscray (Hyde Street) CS	SS – 1877; CS – 1926; Footscray PS (Hyde Street) – 1972; Footscray City PS – 1992
Footscray City College	1. TS and JTS – 1916; New JTS campus (Ballarat Road) – 1943; T College – 1956; Footscray Institute of Technology (FIT) – 1968; TS separates from FIT – 1972; Renamed Footscray City Secondary College – 1982 2. HS – 1954; Renamed Footscray-Yarraville Secondary College – 1992 1 and 2 merged – 1996

Forest Hill College	1. Blackburn South HS – 1959 2. Burwood TS – 1956 3. Burwood Heights HS – 1970 4. Nunawading HS – 1955 1, 2, 3 and 4 merged as Forest Hill SC – 1990; College – 2000
Foster CoS	Opened as Stockyard Creek SS – 1872; HES – 1919; CoS – 1952
Fountain Gate SC, Hallam	Eumemmerring SC – 1990; Fountain Gate SC – 2009
Frankston HS	HS – 1924; Renamed TS – 1952; Renamed HS – 1957
Frankston SDS	Woorinyan Day Training Centre – 1953; Became a government school, Woorinyan SDS – 1976; Renamed Frankston SDS – 1983
Galvin Park SC, Werribee	Werribee TS – 1978; Renamed Galvin Park SC – 1988
Gardenvale CS	1922; PS – 1990
Gardiner CS	SS – 1915; CS – 1916; PS – 1961; Closed – 1992
Geelong HS	Cont – 1910; HS – 1915
Geelong East TS	1958; Renamed James Harrison SC – 1993
Geelong Training Prison	1957
Geelong West TS	JTS – 1954; TS – 1957; Closed – 1987

Gilmore College for Girls, Footscray	Footscray DAS – 1925; GS –1935; GSS – 1950; GHS – 1966; Renamed Gilmore College for Girls – 1996
Gippsland Hospital School, Sale	1944–48
Gisborne HES	1920–33
Gisborne SC	HTS – 1980; SC – 1990
Gladstone Park SC	HS – 1974; SC – 1991
Glenallen School, Glen Waverley	Marathon Spastic Centre – 1952; Glen Waverley Special School – 1980; Glenallen School – early 1990s
Gleneagles SC, Endeavour Hills	Eumemmerring SC – 1995; Gleneagles SC – 2009
Glendonald School for Deaf Children	1951–91

Glen Eira College, Caulfield East	1. Caulfield HS – 1960 2. Caulfield TS – 1968 1 and 2 merged as Caulfield SC – 1987 3. Prahran Mechanics Institute – 1864; Tech Art School – 1909; TS – 1915; Junior Boys' School – 1916; Girls School – 1955; College of Technology – 1967; TS – 1971; Renamed Windsor TS – 1981 4. Ardoch HS – 1978 3 and 4 merged as Ardoch-Windsor SC – 1988 5. Prahran HS – 1965 Ardoch-Windsor SC and 5 merged as Prahran SC – 1989 6. Murrumbeena HS – 1952; SC – 1991 Caulfield SC, Prahran SC and Murrumbeena SC merged as Glen Eira SC – 1996
Glenroy College	1. Glenroy HS – 1954 (see also Ballert Murrup – 1995); SC – 1991 2. Glenroy TS – 1956 3. Hadfield HS – 1964 4. Oak Park HS – 1959; SC – 1990 1, 2, 3 and 4 merged as Box Forest SC – 1993; Renamed Glenroy College – 2010
Glenroy Specialist School	Yooralla Hospital School for Crippled Children – 1922; Yooralla Glenroy (Glenroy Training Centre and Special School) – 1976; Renamed Glenroy SpS – ?
Glenferrie CS, Hawthorn	Manningtree Road SS – 1875; Sloyd Centre and CS – 1906–61; Renamed Glenferrie CS – 1927; PS – 1962

Glen Waverley SC	1. Glen Waverley HS – 1960; SC – 1991 2. Syndal HS – 1967; SC – 1993 3. Syndal TS – 1958; Renamed Lawrence SC – 1991 2 and 3 merged with Glen Waverley SC – 1995
Goongerah P-8 School	PS – 1991; Merged with Tubbut PS as P-8 – 2010
Gordon Institute for Boys, Highett	1951–53
Goroke P-12 College	SS – 1885; GS – 1951; CoS – 1956; P-12 College – 1990
Greensborough SC	1. Watsonia HS – 1962 2. Watsonia TS –1957 1 and 2 merged as Greensborough SC – 1989
Greythorn HS	HS – 1958; Closed – 1991
Grovedale College	THS – 1979; SC – 1990; College – 2002
Gunbower Island CS (also Dalton's Bridge)	1923–48
Gunyah CS	CS – 1907; Closed – 1926; Reopened – 1928; Closed – 1948

Hallam Senior College	HS – 1967; Eumemmerring SC – 1990 Merged with Endeavour Hills SC – 1992 Four campuses disaggregated into four independent colleges – 2009: Endeavour Hills SC (see above) Fountain Gate SC (see above) Gleneagles SC (see above) Hallam Senior College
Hamilton SDS	1989
Hampden Specialist School, Cobden	1. Cooinda Day Training Centre, Terang – ?; Became a government school, Terang SDS – 1989 2. Secondary campus, Cobden TS – 1997 1 and 2 renamed Hampden SpS – 1999
Hampton Convalescent Hospital School	Opened as Hampton Convalescent Home for Children School – 1926; Renamed Hampton Convalescent Hospital School – 1947; Closed – 1959
Hampton Park SC, Dandenong	PPS – 1986; SC – 1990
Harvester Technical College, Sunshine North	Australian Technical College – 2008; Renamed Harvester – 2010 (Campus of Sunshine College, see below)
Hawkesdale P-12 College	HES – 1960; HS – 1962; SC – 1992 Merged with PS – 1994
Hawthorn SC	John Gardiner HS – 1974; SC – 1990; Renamed Hawthorn SC – 1994

Hawthorn West PS	National School – 1853; Hawthorn SS – 1872; CS – 1918; Hawthorn West PS- 1971
Healesville HS	CS – 1952; HS – 1961
Heatherwood School, Donvale	Mitcham SpS – 1962; Renamed Heatherwood School – 1989
Heathcote HES	Common School – 1864; HES – 1921; CS – 1931; HES – 1965; PS – 1965
Heathmont College	1. Mitcham TS – 1954; Renamed Ringwood TS – 1960; Renamed Eastern SC – 1992 2. Heathmont HS – 1976; SC – 1990 1 and 2 merged as Heathmont College – 1992
Heywood and District SC	HS – 1962; Renamed Heywood and District SC – 1990
Heywood Consolidated School	SS – 1880; CoS – 1953
Highvale SC	HS – 1977; SC – 1990
Hillside CS	Moormurng SS – 1876; Hillside SS – 1921; Rosehill PS – 1948
Hillside SpS, Glen Waverley	1958–2000
Hopetoun SC	HES – 1945; HS – 1961; SC – 1988
Hoppers Crossing SC	PPS – 1984; SC – 1988

Horsham College	1. Horsham HS – 1912 2. Horsham TS – 1959 1 and 2 merged as Horsham College – 1994
Horsham SpS	Karkana Day Training Centre – 1972; Became a government school, Horsham SDS – 1988
Hume Central SC, Broadmeadows	1. Broadmeadows HS – 1960; SC – 1990 2. Westmeadows Heights HS – 1978; Renamed Erinbank SC – 1983 3. Broadmeadows West TS – 1967; Hillcrest SC – 1990 1, 2 and 3 merged as Hume Central – 2007
Hume Valley School, Broadmeadows	Broadmeadows and District Helping Hand Association Day Training Centre for Intellectually Impaired Children – ?; Renamed Broadmeadows SpS – 1968; Renamed Broadmeadows SDS – 1987; Renamed Hume Valley School – 2001
Inglewood HES	National School – 1870; Common School – 1871; HES – 1912; PS – 1982
Irymple SC	Mildura South TS – 1968; Renamed Irymple TS – 1972; SC – 1990
Ivanhoe CS	SS – 1881; CS – 1931; PS – 1949
Ivanhoe East CS	SS – 1930; CS – 1933–40; PS – 1941
Jacana School for Autism	Part of the Northern School for Autism – 2006; Demerged to become Jacana School – 2012
Jackson SpS, St Albans	St Albans SpS – 1976; Renamed Jackson School – 1989

Janefield Special School	1937; Closed – ?
Jeparit Primary (CS)	SS – 1889; CS – ?; PS – ?
JH Boyd Girls HS, Southbank	Montague Cookery Centre – 1917; DAS – 1930; JH Boyd DA College – 1932; HS – 1968; Closed – 1985
John Fawkner College	Fawkner HS – 1956; SC – 1989; Renamed College – 2010
John Monash Science School, Clayton	2010
Joseph Banks SC, Doveton	Doveton HS – 1960; SC – 1993; Closed – 2006
Kalianna School, Bendigo	Kangaroo Flat SpS – 1953; Bendigo SpS – 1966; Kalianna – 1976
Kamarook CS	1893–1973
Kambrya College, Berwick	Berwick South SC – 2002; Kambrya College – 2003
Kaniva P-12 College	1. SS – 1883; CoS – 1953 2. HS – 1963; SC – 1989 1 and 2 merged as P-12 – 2002
Katandra School, Ormond	Ormond Special – 1959; Renamed Katandra School – 1992
Keilor SC	Lincolnville HS – 1968; Renamed Keilor HS – 1970; SC – ?

Keilor Downs College	PPS – 1984; SC – 1990; College – 1995
Keilor Heights SC	Keilor Heights HS – 1969; SC – ?; Closed – 1992
Kellalee CS	1901–c.1920s?
Kensington Community HS	1975
Keon Park SC	TS – 1958; SC – ?; Closed – 1992
Kerang THS	HES – 1913; HS – 1919; THS – 1973
Kew East PS	SS – 1892; CS – 1923; PS – 1963
Kew HS	1963
Keysborough College	1. Chandler HS – 1972; SC – 1991 2. Coomoora HS – 1977; SC – 1991 3. Heatherhill HS – 1966; SC – 1990 4. Keysborough TS – 1973; SC – 1990 5. Springvale HS – 1975; SC – 1991 1, 2, 3, 4 and 5 merged as Keysborough Springvale SC – 2008; Renamed Keysborough College – 2009
Kiewa Valley CoS	CoS – 1953; Primary – 1969
Kingsbury SpS	Opened – ?; Closed – 1979
Kingsville (Footscray) CS	CS – 1919–32
Knox SC	TS – 1966; SC – 1990; Closed – 1992

Kooweerup SC	Yallock PS – 1884; Renamed Kooweerup – 1903; CS – 1907; HES – 1953; HS – 1957; SC – 1990
Koonung SC, Mont Albert	Box Hill North HS – 1964; Renamed Koonung HS – 1967; SC – 1990
Korong Vale CS	CS – 1916–45
Korumburra SC	SS – 1891; HES – 1920; HS – 1954; SC – 1990
Kurnai College, Churchill	1. Churchill PPS – 1985 2. Morwell East HS – 1966; Renamed Maryvale HS – 1966 3. Morwell HS – 1956 4. Morwell TS – 1959 1, 2, 3 and 4 merged as Kurnai College – 1987
Kurunjang SC, Melton	PPS – 1986; SC – 1991
Kyabram P-12 College	HES – 1912; HS – 1955; SC – 1989; P-12 College – 2009 with Kyabram PS (Haslem Street) and Kyabram PS (Dawes Road)
Kyneton SC	HS – 1912; THS – 1966; SC – 1990
Lake Bolac College	HES – 1957; HS – 1960; SC – 1990 Lake Bolac PS and SC merged as P-12 College – 1998
Lakes Entrance SC	PPS – 1984; SC – 1990
Lakeview Senior College, Caroline Springs	Caroline Springs College – 2000; Lakeview – 2012

Lalor SC	HS – 1963; SC – 1990
Lalor North SC	HS – 1979; SC – 1990
Lara SC	SC – 2003
Latrobe SDS, Traralgon	?
Lavers Hill P-12 College	Group School – 1953; CoS – 1954; P-12 – 1994
Laverton P-12 College	HS – 1967; SC – 1989 Merged with Laverton Plains PS and Laverton PS as P-12 College – 2008
Leongatha SC	1. AHS – 1913; HS – 1930 2. TS – 1967 1 and 2 merged as SC – 1989
Lilydale Heights College	Lilydale TS – 1970; Lilydale Heights SC – 1989; Renamed Lilydale Heights College – 2004
Lilydale HS	HES – 1919; HS – 1951
Lockington CoS	SS – 1917; CoS – 1953
Lorne-Aireys Inlet P-12 College	1. Airey's Inlet SS – 1893; Closed – 1917; Reopened half-time – 1931; Closed – 1942; Reopened – 1960 2. Lorne SS – 1879; CS – 1957; HES – 1968 1 and 2 merged as Lorne P-12 College – 1994; Renamed Lorne-Airey's Inlet P-12 College – 1997

Lowanna College, Newborough	1. Yallourn TS – 1928; Technical College – 1958 2. Yallourn HES – 1922; HS – 1945 1 and 2 merged as Yallourn SC – 1990 3. Moe HS – 1953; SC – 1990 4. Newborough HS – 1962 Yallourn SC, 3 and 4 merged as Lowanna College – 1994
Lynall Hall Community School, Richmond	Opened as an annex of Brunswick East HS – 1976; Autonomous school – 1983
Lyndale SC, Dandenong North	HS – 1961; SC – 1990
Lyndhurst SC, Cranbourne	Cranbourne Meadows TS – 1980; Lyndhurst SC – 1990
Lysterfield Boys Home	1942–50
MacRobertson GHS, Melbourne	Continuation School – 1907; Renamed Melbourne HS – 1910; Melbourne GHS – 1928; Renamed MacRobertson GHS – 1934
Macleod College	1. Macleod PS – 1928 2. Macleod HS – 1954 1 and 2 merged as P-12 – 1996; Renamed Macleod College – 1998
Maffra SC	HES – 1924; HS – 1955; SC – 1991
Mallacoota P-12 College	SS – 1906; CS – 1965; HES – 1978; P-12 College – 1990

Malmsbury Youth Training Centre	1967; Renamed Malmsbury Youth Justice Centre – 2009
Malvern (Spring Road) CS	Gardiners Creek State School – 1875; Adjunct of Malvern (Tooronga Road) – ?; Resumed the name Gardiner's Creek – 1899; Renamed Malvern CS – 1926
Malvern East CS	1923; PS – after 1970s
Manangatang P-12 College	SS – 1914; HES – 1950; P-12 – 1990
Manor Lakes P-12 Specialist College, Wyndham Vale	Wyndham Vale P-9 Specialist School – ?; Manor Lakes P-12 Specialist College – 2009
Mansfield SC	HS – 1911; HES – 1924; HS – 1962; SC – 1990
Marathon	Opened at SS Armadale – 1950; Relocated to Malvern Road – 1952; Closed – 1979
Marnebek School, Cranbourne	Cranbourne SpS – 2002; Renamed Marnebek School – 2004
Maribyrnong SC	HS – 1958; SC – 1990

Maryborough Education Centre	1. Maryborough HS – 1912 2. Maryborough School of Mines – 1889; Renamed TS – 1903; JTS – 1916; TC – 1958 1 and 2 merged as Maryborough Regional College – 1994 Maryborough Regional College, Maryborough Specialist School (5250) (previously Maryborough SDS from 1986, now Beckworth campus), Maryborough PS (404), and Maryborough East PS 2828 merged as Maryborough Education Centre – 2005
Matthew Flinders Girls SC, Geelong	Flinders Boys Elementary School – 1858; SS – 1880; Mathew Flinders Domestic Arts School – 1940; GSS – 1950; GHS – 1966; Renamed SC – 1989
McLeod Training Centre, French Island	1954–75
McGuire College, Shepparton	Shepparton South TS – 1953; SC – 1991; Renamed McGuire College – 1991
McClelland College, Frankston	1. Ballam Park HS – 1970 2. Ballam Park TS – 1972 1 and 2 merged as Ballam Park SC – 1990 Frankston East HS – 1959; Renamed Karingal Park HS – 1961; SC – 1990 Ballam Park SC and 3 merged as McClelland SC – 1997; Renamed College – 2009

McKinnon SC	HS – 1954; SC – 1988
Meglin SpS	Sutherland Home for Neglected Children – 1909; Sutherland Home School – 1912; Government school – 1968; Renamed Meglin SpS – 1969
Melba College, Croydon	1. Croydon CS – 1953; HS – 1957; SC – 1990 2. Croydon West HS – 1965; Maroondah HS – 1971; SC – 1990 1 and 2 merged as Melba College – 2012
Melbourne Girls College, Richmond	Malvern CS – 1926; GSS – 1945; Malvern DAS merged with GSS – 1946; GHS – 1966; Merged with Melbourne Girls' College – 1994
Melbourne HS	Continuation School – 1907; HS – 1910; BHS – 1928
Melton SC	HS – 1975 TS – 1979 Merged as SC – 1989
Melton Specialist School	?
Mentone Girls SC	Girls' School – 1955; GHS – 1958; SC – 1988
Menzies Boys Home	Ragged Boys Home – 1865; Renamed Minton Boys Home – 1901; Renamed Frankston Boys Home – 1904; School opened – 1922; Renamed Menzies Boys Home School – 1942; Closed – 1961
Merbein CS	1928; Central classes discontinued – 1944; PS – 1945

Merbein P-10 College	HES – 1945; HS – 1960; Merbein SC – 1990; P-10 – 2010 (Merged with Merbein PS, Merbein North PS, Merbein West PS)
Merino CoS	CoS – 1954; PS – 1960
Merriang SDS, Lalor	Whittlesea District Branch, Helping Hand Association – 1971; Merriang SDS – 1989
Middle Park CS	SS – 1887; CS – 1916; PS – 1969
Mildura CS	SS – 1891; CS – ?
Mildura Migrant Centre	1950–52
Mildura Senior College	HS – 1912; SC – 1990; Mildura Senior College – 1995
Mildura Specialist School	?
Mill Park SC	SC – 1991
Mirboo CS	1885–1895
Mirboo North SC	HES – 1922; HS – 1955; SC – 1991
Mitcham SpS	1962; Closed – ?
Mologa CS	CS – 1880; Closed – 1906; Reopened – 1912; Closed – 1962
Monash SC, Clayhton	HS – 1965; SC – pre-1992?; Closed – 2006
Monash SDS, Wheelers Hill	?

Monbulk College	HS – 1963; SC – 1988; College – 1995
Montague CEC, South Melbourne	SS – 1886; Annex of Bell Street Special School – 1915; Became Montague Special School – 1928; Renamed Montague Continuing Education Centre – 1977
Mont Albert CS	PS – 1917; CS – 1918; PS – 1965
Monterey Secondary College	1. Monterey HS – 1966 2. Monterey TS – 1967 1 and 2 merged as SC – 1992
Montmorency SC	HS – 1969; SC – 1989
Moomba Park SC	Fawkner TS – 1960; Renamed Moomba Park SC – 1990; Closed – 1992
Moonee Ponds CS	1919
Moorabbin HS	1962–84
Moorabbin West SpS	1965; Closed – ?
Mooroolbark College	Mooroolbark HS – 1973; Mooroolbark Heights SC – 1990; Mooroolbark College – 2004
Mooroolbark SC	TS – ?; SC – 1991
Mooroopna SC	HS – 1972; SC – 1990

Mordialloc College	Mordialloc District HS – 1924; Renamed Mordialloc Carrum HS – 1924; Renamed Mordialloc-Chelsea HS – 1929; SC – 1990; Renamed Mordialloc College – 2000
Moreland City College	CS – 1947; HS – 1953; Renamed Moreland City College – 1992; Closed – 2004
Moreland PS	SS – 1887; CS – 1926; PS – 1947
Mornington SC	1. CS – 1953; Mornington HS – 1956 2. Mornington North TS – 1980 1 and 2 merged as Mornington SC – 1990
Mornington SDS	Kankama Day Training Centre – ?; Mornington SDS – 1983
Mortlake P-12 College	HES – 1959; HS – 1961; SC – 1992 Merged with Mortlake PS as P-12 – 1994 Caramut PS merged with Mortlake P-12 – 2005
Mount Alexander College, Flemington	Flemington National School – 1858; Flemington Common School – 1862; Flemington SS – 1873–1923; Flemington DAS – 1925; GSS – 1931; GHS – 1966; Debney Park HS – 1973; SC – 1990; Renamed Mount Alexander College – 2012
Mount Beauty SC	HES – 1953; HS – 1963; SC – 1990

Mount Clear College	1. Ballarat Boys TS – 1976 2. Mt Clear TS – 1977 3. Cookery Centre – 1899; Ballarat DAS/ School of Domestic Economy – 1918; GSS – 1936; GHS – 1966; Renamed Mt Clear HS – 1975 1, 2 and 3 merged as Mount Clear SC – 1991; Renamed College – 2001
Mount Eliza SC	HS – 1975; SC – 1990
Mount Erin SC	Baxter TS – 1976; SC – 1991
Mount Evelyn SDS	Melba Centre – ?; Became a government school and named Mount Evelyn SDS – 1985
Mount Ridley P-12 College, Craigieburn	2009
Mount Waverley SC	1. Mount Waverley HS – 1964; SC – 1990 2. Waverly HS – 1956 1 and 2 merged as Mount Waverley SC – 1991
Mullauna College, Mitcham	1. Donvale HS – 1966 2. Mitcham HS – 1959 3. Mitcham TS – 1957 1, 2 and 3 merged as Mullauna SC – 1988; Renamed College – ?
Murrayville Community College	1. PS – 1912; CoS – 1946 2. HS – 1975; Murrayville SC – 1987 1 and 2 merged as Community College – 1994

Murtoa P-12 College	HES – 1922; HS – 1956; SC – 1991 Merged with Murtoa PS (opened in 1875) as P-12 College – 2003
Myrtleford P-12 College	1. SS – 1870; CS – 1927; CoS – 1952; PS – ? 2. HES – 1955; HS – 1960; SC – ? 1 and 2 merged with PS as P-12 – 2009
Naranga School, Frankston	1974
Narre Warren South P-12 College	P-12 – 2002
Nathalia SC	HES – 1919; HS – 1959; SC – 1990
Neerim District SC	Neerim South HES – 1960; HS – 1963; SC – 1990
Nelson Park School, North Geelong	Opened as Geelong Special School – 1968; Renamed Nelson Park School – 1989
Nepean School, Seaford	Royal Children's Hospital School, Hampton – 1925; Royal Children's Hospital School – Mount Eliza – 1929; Nepean School – 1980
Newcomb SC	1. Newcomb HS – 1969; SC – 1989 2. Geelong East TS – 1958; James Harrison SC – ? 1 and 2 merged as Newcomb HS – 2002 Note: Victorian Sailing Water Safety School was established in 1985 and in 2002 amalgamated as part of 1 above.

Newhaven Boys Home	1890; Closed – 1900; Reopened – 1914; Closed – 1926
Newlands SC	HS – 1958; SC – 1991; Closed – 1992
Nhill College	SS – 1881; HES – 1912; HS – 1945; P-12 School – 1979; P-12 College – 1987; Nhill College – 1990
Noble Park English Language School	?
Noble Park SC	1. Noble Park TS – 1957; Renamed Noble Park Heights SC – 1991 2. Noble HS – 1961; SC – 1991 1 and 2 merged as Noble Park SC – 1994
Noble Park SDS	?
Norong CS	1890–1945
Northcote PS (Helen Street)	1874; CS – 1926; PS – 1958
Northern SC, Coburg	1954; Northern SC – 1992; Closed – 1993
North Shepparton SC	Shepparton Technical College – 1953; TS separated – 1981; Renamed North Shepparton SC – 1990; Closed – 1993
North Geelong SC	Geelong North HS – 1966; SC – 2000?
Northcote CS (Helen Street)	SS – 1874; CS – 1925–58; PS – 1959

Northcote HS	HS – 1926; BHS – 1927; HS – 1989
Northern Bay P-12 College, Corio	1. Norlane HS – 1957 2. Norlane TS – 1960; Corio TS – 1960; SC – 1989; Corio Bay Senior College – 1994 3. Corio North HS – 1978; SC – 1990; Renamed Flinders Peak SC – 1991 1, 2 and 3 merged with Corio PS, Corio South PS, Corio West PS, Norlane West PS, North Shore PS and Rosewall PS as Northern Bay College P-12 – 2011
Northern College of the Arts and Tecnology, Preston	Preston TS – 1937; Northland SC – 1991; Closed – 1992; Reopened – 1995; Northern College of the Arts and Technology (Years 10–13) – 2011
Northern School for Autism, East Preston	1. Preston SDS opened – 1980; Merged with Jacana PS and renamed Northern School for Autism – 2006; Relocated to the Reservoir Campus – 2013 2. Jacana SpS merged with Northern – 2006; Demerged to become the Jacana School for Autism – 2013
Norwood SC, Ringwood	HS – 1958; SC – 1991
North Shepparton SC	TS – 1953; SC – 1991; Closed – 1994
Nossal HS, Berwick	2010
Numurkah SC	HES – 1924; HS – 1951; SC – 1990

Nunawading Migrant Centre School	1950–52
Oakleigh Senior College	TS – 1946; SC – 1991; Senior College closed – 1992
Oakleigh HS	HS – 1955; Closed – 1992
Oberon HS, Belmont	1963
Officer SpS	2014
Orbost SC	HES – 1912; HS – 1948; SC –1990
Ouyen P-12 College	HES – 1929; HS – 1952; SC – 1987; Merged with Ouyen PS as P-12 – 2008
Pakenham Cons	1953
Pakenham SC	HS – 1968; SC – 1991
Parkdale SC	HS – 1964; SC – 1990
Parkwood SC, North Ringwood	HS – 1979; SC – 1991
Pascoe Vale Girls College	GSS – 1956; GHS – 1966; SC – 1991; College – 2002
Patchewollock GS	1918; Discontinued post primary classes – 1968

Patterson River SC, Seaford	1. Seaford HS – 1967; Renamed Seaford Carrum High School – 1968; SC – 1991 2. Bonbeach HS – 1957 1 and 2 merged as Patterson River SC – 1992
Payika College A Koorie Pathways School, Swan Hill	Payika College – ?; Swan Hill Koorie Pathways School – ?; Victoria P-12 College of Koorie Education – 2006
Peninsula Specialist College, Dromana	?
Pentridge Penal Establishment School	1924–97
Peter Lalor SC, Lalor	Lalor TS – 1968; Peter Lalor SC – 1991; Renamed Peter Lalor Vocational College (Years 10–12) – 2011
Phoenix P-12 Community College, Sebastapol	Sebastapol GTS – 1961; TS – 1961; SC – 1990; Ballarat South Community Learning Precinct – 2011; Phoenix – 2012
Pleasant Street CS, Ballarat	Elementary Classes – 1914; HES – 1915; CS – 1919; Annex – Ballarat HS (the Branch) – 1940; Special School – 1953; Ballarat PS (Pleasant Street) – 1963; Pleasant Street PS (Ballarat) – 2000
Point Cook P-9 College	PS (RAAF Base) – 1923; P-9 – 2010

Point Cook Senior SC	2008
Police Depot School	Police Depot School – 1929; Renamed – ?
Poowong CS	PS – 1878; CS – 1941; GS – 1949; CoS – 1957; Post primary classes closed – 1971
Portarlington HES	SS – 1885; HES – 1924; PS – 1933
Port Fairy CoS	Belfast SS – 1873; Port Fairy HES – 1925; Cos – 1949
Portland SC	1. Portland HES – 1912; HS – 1945 2. Portland TS – 1970 1 and 2 merged as SC – 1992
Portland SpS	?
Port Phillip Specialist School, Port Melbourne	?
Post Primary School, Ballarat	Dana Street – 1939; Humffray Street – 1946
Preston East TS	1960–85
Preston Technical College	TS – 1937; Girls JTS added – 1956; Boys JTS (Jessie Street) – ?; Technical College – 1964; Institute of Technology – 1967; Technical College separated from the Institute – 1970?
Preston Girls SC	DAS and HS – 1928; GS – 1935; GSS – 1949; GHS – 1958; SC – 1989; Closed – 2013

Princes Hill SC	SS – 1889; CS – 1944; HS – 1959; SC – 1988
Pyramid Hill College	SS – 1875; CS – 1961; HES – 1975; College – 1990
Quambatook GS	SS – 1909; GS – 1948; Discontinued Post primary Classes – 1968
Rainbow SC	HES – 1919; HS – 1959; SC – 1988
Red Cliffs SC	CS – 1937; HS – 1961; SC – 1992
Red Hill CoS	CoS – 1950; Postprimary classes ended – 1969
Reservoir HS	1. Reservoir HS – 1954; SC – 1988 2. Kingsbury TS – 1967; SC – 1991 3. Preston East HS – 1964 1, 2 and 3 merged as Reservoir District SC – 1992; HS – 2011
Richmond Central	SS – 1875; CS – 1905; PS – 1955; Closed – 1987
Richmond GHS	Richmond GSS – 1954; GHS – 1969; Closed – 1988
Richmond SC	1. Richmond TS – 1926 2. Richmond HS – 1967 1 and 2 merged as SC – 1990; Closed – 1992
Ringwood SC	HS – 1954; SC – 1991
Robinvale P-12 College	1. HS – 1957; SC – 1988 2. SS – 1925; Consol – 1950; 1 and 2 merged as P-12 College – 2010

Rochester SC	HES – 1920; HS – 1957; SC – 1991
Rosamond School, Maidstone	Footscray North SpS – 1943; Renamed Rosamond SpS – 1980?
Rosebud SC	Red Hill Central Classes – 1952 HS – 1954; SC – 1989
Rosehill SC, Niddrie	Niddrie TS – 1959; Merged as part of Essendon – Keilor SC – 1990; Niddrie SC – 1991; Rosehill SC – 2007
Rowville SC	1989
Roxburgh College	2003
Royal Children's Hospital School	Hampton Convalescent Hospital School – 1925; Relocated to Royal Children's Hospital – 1927
Royal Park Girls Special School	1955–59
Rubicon Outdoor Centre, Thornton	1978
Rupanyup CS	SS – 1878; CS – ?; PS – ?
Rushworth Migrant Centre School	1949–52
Rushworth P-12 College	HES – 1921; HS – 1961; SC – 1990 Merged with Rushworth PS as P-12 College – 1996
Rutherglen HS	HES – 1912; HS – 1961; SC – 2001; HS – ?

Rutherglen PS	HES – 1967; PS – ?
Sale College	1. Sale AHS – 1907; HS – 1917 2. Sale TS – 1885; Renamed Macalister SC – 1991 1 and 2 merged as Sale College – 1996
Sale Specialist School	?
Salvation Army Boys Home (The Basin) Bayswater	Bayswater Boys' Home – 1897; Department school – 1923; Bayswater Youth Training Centre – ?; Bayswater Boys' Home – ?; Bayswater Farm and Vocational Training Centre – ?; Salvation Army Farm and Training Centre – ?; Closed – 1987
Salvation Army Boys School, Box Hill	Department school – 1923; Secondary section closed – 1956
Salvation Army Girls Home	Department school – 1922; Closed – 1949
Sandringham College	1. Beaumaris HS – 1958 2. Hampton HES – 1921; HS – 1935 3. Highett HS – 1956 4. Sandringham TS – 1949 1, 2, 3 and 4 merged as Sandringham SC – 1988, College – 2002
Scoresby SC	HS – 1975; SC – 1990
Seymour P-12 College	HES – 1919; HS – 1948; THS – 1974; P-12 College – 2010 (merged with Seymour PS, Seymour East PS and Seymour Special School)
Shepparton CS	CS – 1876; Closed – 1909

Shepparton HS	AHS – 1909; HS – 1917
Sherbroke Community School	1985
Skene Street SpS, Stawell	1. Pleasant Creek Training Centre – 1937; Pleasant Creek Special School – ? 2. Biala SDS – 1977 1 and 2 merged as Stawell SDS – 1987; Renamed Skene Street School – 1994; Closed – 1999
Somers Migrant Centre School	1949–57
Somerton SC	Broadmeadows TS – 1962; Renamed Somerton SC – 1991; Closed – 1992
Somerville SC	1. Somerville PPP – ?; Closed – 2003 2. Somerville SC – 2009
South Barwon SC	Geelong TS – 1913; South Barwon SC – 1991; Closed – 1996
Southern Autistic School, East Bentleigh	Mentone Special School – 1975; Became a government school – 1986; Relocated and renamed Southern Autistic School – 2002
South Gippsland SC, Foster	HS – 1952; Renamed SGSC – 1990
South Gippsland Specialist School, Leongatha	?

South Oakleigh SC	A. Huntingdale HS – 1959 B. 1. Clayton TS – 1961 2. Huntingdale TS – 1972 1 and 2 merged as Clayton – Huntingdale SC – 1991 C. Moorleigh HS – 1966; SC – ? A, B and C merged as South Oakleigh SC – 1993; Renamed College – 2003 (unofficial)
Springvale Park SDS	Urrimbirra Day Training Centre – 1974; Renamed Springvale and Noble Park Centre for the Mentally Handicapped – 1974; Became a government school and renamed Noble Park SDS – 1984; Renamed Springvale Park SDS – 2013
Springvale TS	Post-1972?; Closed – 1989
Springside P-9 College, Caroline Springs	Caroline Springs College – 2000; Springside – 2012
St Albans SC	HS – 1956; SC – 1989
St Albans Park HS	HS – 1970; SC – ?
St Arnaud SC	HES – 1912; HS – 1914; SC – 1990
St Helena SC, Eltham North	PPS – 1984; SC – 1988
Staughton College, Melton	Melton TS – 1979; Renamed Wilson Park SC – 1988; College – 2003

Stawell SC	1. SS – 1878; Closed – 1911; Reopened as Stawell HS – 1912 2. Stawell School of Mines – 1882; JTS (Technical College) – 1916 1 and 2 merged as SC – 1987
Strathmore SC	HS – 1957; SC – 1991
Sunbury & Macedon Ranges Specialist School, Jacksons Hill	?
Sunbury SC	HS – 1960; SC – 1990; College – 2003
Sunbury Downs College	Sunbury PPS – 1988; Sunbury Downs SC – 1990
Sunshine College	1. Sunshine TS – 1913 2. Sunshine HS – 1955 3. Annex of Sunshine TS – 1977; Ardeer HS – 1979; SC – 1990 4. Sunshine North TS – 1960; SC – 1990 5. Sunshine West HS – 1960 6. Tottenham TS – 1957 1, 2, 3, 4, 5, and 6 merged as Sunshine College – 1992 with campuses 2 and 6 closing
Sunshine SDS	Sunshine House Day Training Centre – ?; Became a government school and renamed Sunshine SDS – 1985

Surf Coast Secondary College, Torquay	2012
Surrey Hills PS	1886; Unofficial central classes – 1927–33
Suzanne Cory HS, Werribee	2011
Swan Hill College	1. Rural School – 1871; PS – 1872; HES – 1919; Closed – 1977 2. HS – 1928 3. TS – 1961 2 and 3 merged as SC – 1992; Renamed College – 2000
Swan Hill Specialist School	Lady Byrnes Centre – ?; SDS – 1987; Renamed Swan Hill SpS – 2001?
Swifts Creek P-12 College	1. SS – 1874; Swifts Creek Central Classes – 1955; HES – 1964; Consolidated – 2. Omeo SS – 1866; HES – 1912; CS – 1914; Central classes – 1956; HES – 1964; PS – 1978 1 and 2 merged as Swifts Creek HS – 1978; SC – ? 3. Swifts Creek SS – 1874; PS – 1978 3 and Swifts Creek SC merged as Swifts Creek P-12 College – 2010
Swinburne Senior SC	Eastern Suburbs Technical College – 1908; Renamed Swinburne Technical College – 1913 with Boys Junior Technical School; Girls Junior Technical School – 1916; Coeducational Swinburne Technical School – 1968; Senior TS – 1972; Swinburne Senior SC – 1993

Swinburne Community School	1972–89
Sydney Road Community School	1986
Talbot Colony for Epileptics, Masonmeadows	Colony – 1907; School – 1914; Closed – 1962
Tallangatta SC	HES – 1959; HS – 1961; SC – 1990
Tally Ho Boys Home school	1908–86
Tamleugh CS	1918–27
Taylors Lakes SC	1991
Templestowe College	1. Templestowe HS – 1960 2. Templestowe TS – 1971; Yarra SC – 1993 1 and 2 merged as Templestowe College – 1994
Terang College	1. HES – 1927; HS – 1950; 5–12 Campus – 2005 2. National School – 1858; Common School – 1862; SS – 1872; HES – 1924; PS – 1950; P-4 Campus – 2005 1 and 2 merged as P-12 College – 1996
The Grange P-12 College, Hoppers Crossing	Werribee-Grange SC – 1993; Renamed P-12 College – 1998

The Lakes South Morang P-9 School	2007
Thomastown SC	HS – 1957; SC – 1990
Thornbury HS	1. Thornbury HS – 1962; SC – 1990 2. Northcote TS – 1966; Renamed Darebin Parklands SC – 1989 1 and 2 merged as Thornbury – Darebin SC – 1992; Renamed Thornbury HS – 2005
Timboon P-12 School	1. SS – 1883; CoS – 1948 2. HS – 1960 1 and 2 merged as P-12 – 1995
Tongala East PS	SS – 1875; CoS – 1945; PS – ?
Toolamba CS	SS – 1876; CS – 1912; PS – ?; Closed – 1994
Toorak CS	Toorak PS – 1890; CS – 1919; PS – 1991; Closed – ?
Tormore SC	Boronia HS – 1957; Renamed Tormore SC – 1991; Closed – 1991
Torquay College	PS – 1900; P-9 College – 2009; P-6 College – 2012
Tottenham Community SC	TS – 1957; Community SC – 1991; Closed – 1992
Trafalgar HS	1963

Traralgon College	1. HES – 1915; HS – 1951 2. Traralgon TS – 1960; Traralgon Heights SC – 1990 1 and 2 merged as Traralgon SC – 1993; Renamed College – ?
Travancore School, Flemington	SpS – 1933; Centre for emotionally disturbed children – 1968; Centre for Young People's Mental Health – 1994; Community Group Program – 1995; Travancore School Outreach Team – 2008
Two Rivers College A Koorie Pathways School, Mildura	Chaffey KODE Campus – 1998; Mildura Campus of Victorian P-12 College of Koorie Education – 2006; Two Rivers – 2009
Tyntynder CS	CS – 1913; PS – 1951; Closed – 1992
Tyrrell College, Sewa Lake	Sea Lake HES – 1920; HS – 1962; SC – 1988; Merged with Sea Lake PS to form Tyrell P-12 College – 1994
University HS	University Practising School – 1910; HS – 913
Upfield SC	HS – 1966; SC – 1990; Closed – 2010
Upper Yarra SC	Warburton CS – 1953; HES – 1958; HS – 1961; HTS – 1981; SC – 1990
Upwey HS	HES – 1937; HS – 1945
Vectis Central	1890–96
Vermont SC	HS – 1963; SC – 1990
Vermont South SpS	Burwood East SpS – 1973; Renamed Vermont South SpS – 1973

Verney Road School, Shepparton	1. Graham Street SpS – 1978 2. Shepparton SDS attached to Goulburn Valley Day Training Centre – 1980; Goulburn SDS – 1983 1 and 2 merged as Verney Road School – 1999
Victorian College for the Deaf, Melbourne	Victorian Deaf and Dumb Institution – 1860; Victorian School for Deaf Children – 1949; Renamed Victorian College for the Deaf – 1995
Victoria University SC, Junior Campus – Deer Park, Senior Campus – St Albans	1. St Albans TS – 1962; Jamieson Park SC – 1990; Brimbank College – 1998 2. Deer Park HS – 1972; SC – 1990 1 and 2 merged as Victoria University SC – 2010 3. Kealba HS – 1970; SC – 1990 3 merged with Victoria University SC – 2011
Victorian College Of The Arts Secondary School, Melbourne	1977
Victorian Railways TS, Newport	1923; Closed – 1979; Became part of the Newport College of TAFE – 1982
Victorian School of Languages	1935
Viewbank College	1. Banyule HS – 1961 2. Rosanna East HS – 1970 1 and 2 merged as College – 1994

Vision Australia School	Victorian Asylum and School for the Blind – 1868; Renamed RVIB – 1891; Vision Australia School – ?
Waitchie CS	CS – 1912; Closed – 1951
Wallan SC	2006
Wanganui Park SC, Shepparton	Shepparton GSS – 1960; GHS – 1966; Renamed Wanganui HS – 1975; SC – 1990
Wangaratta District Specialist School	Wangaratta SDS – 1986; Renamed Wangaratta District SpS – 1995
Wangaratta HS	1. AHS – 1909; HS – 1921 2. TS – 1927; JTS – 1955; SC – 1991; Ovens College – 1999 1 and 2 merged – 2007
Wantirna College	HS – 1980; SC – 1990; College – 1998
Wantirna Heights School	?
Waratah SDS, West Heidelberg	Milparinka Day Training Centre – ?; Became a government school and renamed Milparinka SDS – 1976; Renamed Brunswick SDS – 1984; Relocated and renamed as Waratah SDS – 2011
Warracknabeal SC	HES – 1912; HS – 1924; SC – 1989
Warracknabeal SDS	Opened as Woodbine Day Training Centre – 1954; Renamed Warracknabeal SDS – 1990

Warragul & District Specialist School	?
Warragul Regional College	1. Warragul AHS – 1911; HS – 1917 2. Warragul TS – 1959; SC – 1991 1 and 2 merged as Warragul Regional College – 1994
Warrandyte HS	1978
Warrnambool College	1. AHS – 1907; HS – 1917; SC – 1990 2. Warrnambool North TS – 1968; SC – 1990 1 and 2 merged as Warrnambool College – 1994
Warrnambool SDS	Yalundah Day Training Centre – ?; Warrnambool SDS – 1989
Warringa Park School, Hoppers Crossing	Werribee Shire Centre for Mentally Retarded Children (Wyndham School) – 1975; Became a government school, Wyndham Special School – 1977; Renamed Hoppers Crossing SDS – 1981; Hoppers Crossing SDS – 1998; Warringa Park School – 2000
Wattle Park SC	HS – 1962; SC – 1990; Closed – 1992
Waverley SC	HS – 1956; SC – 1990; Closed – 1991
Wedderburn P-12 College	HES – 1945; HS – 1961; P-12 – 1999

Weeroona College Bendigo	1. School of Mines and Industries – 1873; White Hills STS – 1961; SC – 1989 2. Bendigo East PS – 1916 1 and 2 merged as White Hills P-10 – 1999; Renamed Weeroona College – 2000
Wellington SC, Mulgrave	HS – 1973; SC – 1990
Werribee SC	HES – 1921; HS – 1957; SC – 1988
Werrimull P-12 School	PS – 1925; GS – 1948; CoS – 1968; P-12 – 1996
Westall English Language Centre	?
Westall SC	HS – 1963; SC – 1990
Westall TS	Post-1956?
Western Autistic School, Niddrie	1. Day Training Centre – 1980; Became a government school and named Western Autistic Centre – 1990; Renamed Western Austistic School – 1995
Western English Language School P-10, Braybrook	?

Western Heights College, Geelong North	1. Bell Park HS – 1959 2. Geelong West TS – 1954 1 and 2 merged as Western Heights SC – 1988 3. Bell Park TS –1968 3 amalgamated with Western Heights SC – 1994 Renamed Western Heights College – 1994 (unofficial)
Western Port SC, Hastings	Hastings HS – 1974; Western Port SC – 1991
Westgarth CS	CS – 1924; PS – 1967
Wheelers Hill SC	HS – 1980; SC – 1990
Whitehorse TS	Box Hill GTS – 1924; Whitehorse TS – 1971; Whitehorse TAFE – 1981
Whittlesea SC	THS – 1977; SC – 1989
William Ruthven Secondary College, Reservoir	1. Lakeside HS – 1962; SC – ? 2. Merrilands HS – 1957; SC – 1991 1, 2 and 3 merged as William Ruthven SC – 2010
Williamstown HS	1. HS – 1915 2. Williamstown DAS – 1925; GSS – 1950; GHS – 1966; Renamed Point Gellibrand HS – 1973; GHS – 1988; SC – 1992; Merged with Williamstown HS – 2001
Winchelsea HES	Common School – 1871; SS – 1878; CS – c.1922; HES – 1964; PS – 1984

Winlaton Special School, Nunawading	Royal Park Girls Special School opened – 1955; Closed – 1959; Winlaton opened – 1959
Wodonga Middle Years College	1. Wodonga West HS – 1976; SC – 1991 2. Wodonga TS – 1968; Renamed Mitchell SC – 1992 1 and 2 merged as Wodonga Middle Years College – 2006
Wodonga Senior SC	Belvoir National School – 1852; Wodonga National School – 1869; CS – 1923; HES – 1938; HS – 1954; Renamed Wodonga Senior SC – 2006
Wonthaggi SC	1. HES – 1933; HS – 1967 2. TS – 1922; THS – 1965 1 and 2 merged as SC – 1988
Wonyip CS	CS – 1908; Renamed Ryton – 1909; Closed – 1941
Woolum Bellum College – A Koorie Pathways School, Morwell	Kurnai College – KODE (Koorie Open Door Education) – 1995; Became Woolum Bellum College – 2009
Woomelang Group School	1900–46
Wycheproof P-12 College	1. National School – 1876; Central classes – 1913; PS – ? 2. HES – 1928; HS – 1975 1 and 2 merged with PS to form P-12 – 1990
Yallourn HS	HES – 1929; HS – 1945; Closed – 1978

Yallourn SC	TS – 1928; TC – 1958; TS – 1982; SC – 1990; Closed – 1993
Yarrabah School, Aspendale	Yarrabah Day Training Centre – 1974; Became a government school, Yarrabah SDS – 1976; Renamed Yarrabah School – 1983
Yarra Hills SC, Moorolbark	1. Mooroolbark TS – 1962; Renamed SC – 1990 2. Pembroke HS – 1968; SC – 1989 1 and 2 merged as Pembroke SC – 1994 3. Mt Evelyn TS – 1979; SC – 1990; Merged with Pembroke SC – 1995 Pembroke SC renamed Yarra Hills SC – 2011
Yarram SC	HES – 1919; HS – 1951; SC – 1991
Yarrawonga College P-12	HES – 1919; HS – 1954; SC – 1990; Merged with PS as P-12 – 2010
Yarraville SDS	?
Yea HS	SS – 1860; HES – 1922; HS – 1956
Yooralla Hospital School for Crippled Children, Carlton	1918 See also Belmore School, Glenallen School, Glenroy Specialist School
Yuille Park P-8 Community College, Ballarat	2008

Sources

Blake, Leslie (Gen. ed.) (1973), *Vision and Realisation: A centenary history of state education in Victoria*, Vols 2 and 3, Melbourne, Education Department.

Education Department, Annual Reports, 1900–2015.

Education Department, *Education Gazette and Teachers' Aid, 1900–92. Individual schools as listed above.*

Does Your School Have a History? – Print and Web Histories

In this celebratory history of government secondary education we have focused on many common elements in that history and showcased the history of a sample of those schools. Many schools have already recorded their own history, often in association with an important milestone in their story – a significant anniversary, the opening of new buildings or as a merger with other schools was about to happen. These histories have been written, acknowledging the thousands of students that have passed through each school's door, the hundreds of teachers who taught and inspired them and the thousands of parents who supported them and their school in a rich variety of ways. Those histories take several forms – commercial publications, in-house booklets and as part of the school's website. Known works are listed below.

School histories which can be purchased from the school are identified next to the school's name by (P) and those that can be read at the school are marked (R).

If your school has not already started to record its history, you might want to consider getting a group of people together to collect the records, make sense of them and record that history while people are still around to share their memories of school days. Every government school has a great story to tell of its contributions to its community, Victorian and national life as well as to the lives of its students, teachers and parents. These achievements should be celebrated and the challenges faced acknowledged.

School	History
Altona North Technical School	Pearson, K.F. (Kevin F.), *And ANTS It Was: A History of Altona North Technical School*, Altona North Technical School, 1992
Ararat High School	Jones, A. B., *Ararat High School Jubilee, 1913–1963*, Ararat High School Jubilee Committee, 1963
Bairnsdale High School	*Bairnsdale High School 75th Anniversary 1987*, pamphlet, Bairnsdale High School, 1987
Bairnsdale Technical School	Prendergast, Lorna, *Scatter the Light: A Century of Technical Education in Bairnsdale, 1890–1990*, East Gippsland Community College of TAFE, 1990
Ballarat High School	Cotton, Helen, *The History of the Ballarat High School 1907–1947*, Ballarat High School, n.d. 1947? Roberts, Phillip, *Duty Always: The History of Ballarat High School, 1907–1982*, Ballarat High School, 1982 Philip Roberts, *High School, A Hundred Years, Thousands of Footsteps,* Mud Group, Geelong, 2007
Ballarat Special School	Blythman, Marion, *50 Special Years: The History of the Special School in Ballarat: 1955–2005*, Ballarat Special School, 2005
Ballarat Technical School	Murray, Kevin, *A History of the Ballarat Technical School,* Waller & Chester, 1969

Balwyn High School (P)	Bourke, Valerie, Murray, Peter Craigie et al., *Our Tribute to Our High School: A History of Balwyn High School 1954–2004: Fifty Years of Excellence in State Education*, Balwyn High School, 2004
Belmont High School	Morris, Allan, *The First Twenty-Five Years, 1955–1979: A Very Short History of Belmont High School*, Belmont Press, 1980 Swan, A.E., *Strive for the Highest: The Belmont High School Story, 1955–1995*, Belmont High School, 1995
Benalla High School (P)	Watt, Bruce, *A History of Benalla High School, 1912–1987*, Benalla High School, 1987
Benalla College	*Our schools: Celebrating the First Hundred Years of Public Secondary Education in Benalla*, 2012
Bendigo High School/Bendigo Senior Secondary College (P)	Bomford, Janette M., *The School on the Hill 1907–1982*, Cambridge Press, 1982 Bomford, Janette M., *The School on the Hill 1907–1997*, Richard Cambridge Printers Pty Ltd, 1997 Bomford, Janette M., *The School on the Hill 1907–2007*, Richard Cambridge Printers Pty Ltd, 2007
Bentleigh Secondary College (R)	Eldridge, Sandra, *Bentleigh Secondary College: A History 1950s to 2002*, Bentleigh SC, 2002
Blackburn High School (R)	Barton, Ken, *Blackburn High School: 25 Years*, Blackburn High School, 1980
Boisdale Consolidated School	Montague, Helen, *Fields of Learning – A History of the Consolidation of Seven Rural Schools*, JJB Publishing, 2001

Box Hill Boys' Junior Technical School	Shand, Ian Donald, *The Establishment of the Box Hill Boys Junior Technical School*, Box Hill College of TAFE, 1981?
Box Hill High School (R)	Wiencke, Shirley W., *Box Hill High School Jubilee*, Box Hill High School, 1980
Braybrook College	Habgood, Kate et al., *Braybrook College: 50th Anniversary 1960–2010*, pamphlet, Braybrook College, 2010
Broadmeadows Secondary College	*Broadmeadows High School: Glimpses of the Past*, Broadmeadows Secondary College, 1991 *Winds of Change: Broadmeadows Secondary College: Forty Years*, CD-ROM, Broadmeadows Secondary College, c.2000
Brunswick Secondary College	Eckersall, Kenneth Eric, *Lifelong Learning: A History of Brunswick Secondary College and the Former Brunswick Technical School and of Brunswick: A Microcosm of Australia's National, Social and Cultural History*, Kenneth Eric Eckersall, Brunswick Secondary College, 2009
Buckley Park College (R)	Mary, Bergin, *Buckley Park High School Buckley Park Secondary College Buckley Park College: The story of a Community*, Buckley Park College, 2003
Camberwell High School	Ewins, Robert, *Camberwell High School 1941–1991: A Jubilee Retrospective*, Messenger, 1991
Cann River P-12 College	*Township of Cann River, Parish of Noorinbee, County of Croajingolong, Shire of Orbost (50th Anniversary of Cann River P-12 College)*, Cann River P-12 College, 1977

Canterbury Girs' Secondary College	Rumbold, Margaret E., *These Our School Days: Mangarra Road Revisited*, Canterbury Girls' Secondary College, 2000 Francis, Rosemary et al., *Doing Something More, Feeling Important and Privileged: Members of the first Matriculation Class at Canterbury Girls' Secondary College Recall the Years 1953–58*, Spectrum Print Solutions, 2011
Casterton High School	Lawrence, Graeme, *Casteron High School: The First Years*, Border Watch Print, n.d. 1979?
Castlemaine High School	*History of the Castlemaine High School: 75th Anniversary, 1910–1975*, Castlemaine Mail, 1985
Caulfield North Primary School	*80th Anniversary Commemorative Yearbook, 1914–1994: Caulfield North Primary School (Formerly Central School)*, Employ Publishing Group, 1994
Charlton High School	Cadzow, Grace (Compiler), *Charlton High School: the First Twenty-Five Years*, Creative Rural Printers, 1988
Cohuna Secondary College	Bottcher, Jenny, Dale, Geoff (Editors), *Meandering Memories: Fifty Years of History and Memories, Cohuna High School 1955–1991, Cohuna Secondary College 1991–2005*, Cohuna Secondary College, c.2005
Colac High School	History Faculty, Colac High School, *A Short History of Colac High School, Formerly the Colac Agricultural High School, to Mark Its 75th Anniversary, 1911–1986*, Colac High School, 1986
Collingwood College	Young, John, *The School on the Flat: Collingwood College: 1882–2007*, Collingwood College, 2007

Corryong High School	*Corryong High School Silver Jubilee, 1853–1978*, pamphlet, Corryong High School, 1978
Dandenong High School	Mitchell, K.B. et al., *A History of the Dandenong High School 1919–1968*, Dandenong High School Advisory Council, 1968
Dandenong Technical School	Hellyer Ina, *Dandenong Technical School 30th Anniversary Hub, 1954–1984*, Dandenong Technical School, 1984
Daylesford Technical High School	Darwin, Norm, *A Unique School: 100 years of Secondary Schooling in Daylesford*, Daylesford Technical High School Council, 1990
Eaglehawk High Technical School	Badman, Wendy, *Eaglehawk High Technical School: 25 years 1964–1989*, Eaglehawk High Technical School, 1989
Eltham High School	Thomas, Greg, Whiteley, Robert et al., *Eltham High School a State Secondary College 1926–90*, Eltham High School, 1990/91? Max Balchin, *Eltham High School, A History, 1926–1978*, Eltham High School, 1978/79?
Essendon High School	*Silver jubilee, 1913–1938, Essendon High School*, Don Printing Works, 1938 *Essendon High School: 75th Anniversary 1913–1988*, pamphlet, Essendon High School?, 1988?
Essendon Technical School	*Essendon Technical School, 50 Years 1938–1988: Vulcan's Jubilee Edition*, Universal Printing Services, 1988

Euroa High School	Ludeke, B.A.P., *25 Great Years – A Brief History of Euroa High School – 1956–1981*, Euroa High School, 1981 Brian & Heather Bamford, Di Mackrell, Wendy Humphrey and Paul Rieusset, *Silver to Gold 1981–2006: The Next 25 years,* Euro Printers, 2006
Ferntree Gully College	*Ferntree Gully College: 'The End of an Era'*, Ferntree Gully College, 2006
Footscray Girls' Secondary College	Gallo, Carmela, *As Time Goes by: An Oral History of Footscray Girls' Secondary College*, Gilmore College for Girls, 1997 *Footscray Girls' High School: Our First 60 Years 1925–1985*, Footscray Girls' Secondary College, 1985
Frankston High School	Evans, Mary A., Murray, Heather & Evans, Jenny, *Optima Semper: A History of Frankston High School, 1924–1994*, Frankston High School Council, Brown Prior Anderson Pty Ltd, Burwood, 1995
Heatherton Central/Primary School	*150 Years of Education in Heatherton: The Full Circle 1853–2003*, Snap Printing, 2003
Huntingdale High School	Bereznicki,_Barbara, *Huntingdale High School: Silver Jubilee 1959–1984*, Huntingdale High School, 1984
Jordanville Technical School	*Jordanville Technical School, Pride in Achievement: Silver Jubilee, 1954–1979*, Jordanville Technical School, 1979
Kaniva High School	*Kaniva High School: I serve, 25*, pamphlet, Kaniva High School, 1988

Kerang High School	Gardener, J. Graham, *A History of Kerang High School 1919–1969*, Kerang New Times, 1969
Kerang Technical High School	Gardener, Graham, *Looking Back: A History of Kerang and Its Historic Technical High School 1919–2009*, Lake Bolac, Self-published, 2009
Kew High School (P)	Bourke, Valerie, Brown, Bruce and Morrissey, Sylvia, *Aspire, Strive, Achieve, the Kew High Story 1963–2013*, Self-published, 2013
Kooweerup High School	Hooper, F.C. & Wah, David, *The Tale of the Black Fish: A History of the Kooweerup High School (1957–77)*, Kooweerup High School, 1979
Korumburra Secondary College	Collyer, Richard, *Korumburra Secondary College 1954–2008: A Chronicle*, Korumburra Secondary College, c.2008
Kyneton High School (R)	Bremner, G.A. (George Alexander), *Onward and Upward: Kyneton High School Diamond Jubilee, 1912–1972*, Kyneton Guardian, 1972 *Columns,* Centenary edition, Kyneton Secondary College, 2012 (P)
Lakes Entrance Post Primary School	Freestone, Gerry, Davis, Jan, *Lakes Entrance Post Primary School,* Lakes Entrance Post Primary School, 1984
Leongatha SC	Skillern, Lynette, *En avant: Leongatha High School, 1912–1987*, Leongatha High School, 1987 Skillern, Lyn et al., *From Inkwell to Internet: A Century of State Secondary Education in Leongatha,* Leongatha Secondary College, 2012

MacRobertson Girls' High School	Honey, Ennis, *Nymphs and Goddesses: The Story of a Girlhood*, Beaufort Books, Balgowlah NSW, 1994 Sherson, Susan, *Always Your Voice Will Call*, MacRobertson Girls' High School, 1994 Parker, Pauline, *The Making of Women: A History of MacRobertson Girls' High School*, Melbourne, Australian Scholarly Publishing, 2006
Malvern Central School	*Your Final Year, 1930–1949: Who Returned to Spring Road School in 1975*, manuscript, Malvern Central School, 1975 Wiencke, Shirley Winsome, *Malvern and the Spring Road School: A Short History*, Malvern Central School, 1975
Manangatang P-12 College (R)	*Moondah State School No. 4223, 1925–1946,* A compilation of collected memoirs, 1946? Smith, Robert M., *Now There Are Six – An Historical Overview of Education in the Manangatang Area,* A compilation of collected memoirs, 1980 May, B. A., *75 Years of Education in Manangatang, 1924–1989,* Local history class project, 1989
Mansfield High School	Cole, Sandra, Gear, Patricia (eds.), *Mansfield High School 25th Anniversary 1987*, Mansfield High School, 1987 Barr, Lynton G. *Mansfield High School: The Foundation Years 1962–1968,* Mansfield High School, 2012
Maryborough High School	*Maryborough High School 1912–1987*, Maryborough High School, 1987

Maryborough Technical School	Barber, G.W. & Williams, J.M., *100 Years at the Maryborough Technical College,* The Book Printer, Maryborough, 1988
Matthew Flinders Girls' Secondary College	Hooper, Anne, *The Story of Flinders School, Geelong, 1856–1956,* Mercer Press, Geelong, 1956 McNair, Dorothy, Vines, Heather M., *Daughters of Australia: The Story of Matthew Flinders: A School for Girls 1940–1995,* Geelong, 1995
Melbourne High School	Hocking, J., *Story of Melbourne High School, 1905–1921*, Specialty Press, 1922 Inch, Allen, *Honour the Work: A History of Melbourne High School*, Lloyd O'Neil, 1977 Gregory, Alan, *Strong Like Its Pillars Melbourne High School 1905–2005: Victoria's First State Secondary School*, Brown Prior Anderson, Melbourne, 2005
Mentone Girls' Secondary College	Cerni, Patricia, *The Evolution of a Girls' School: A Celebration of the 40th Anniversary of Mentone Girls' Secondary College 1955–1995*, Mentone Girls' Secondary College, 1995
Mildura High School	Miller, Glen (ed.), *The School We Knew: The Best School of All: Personal Recollections of Mildura High School 1912–1987,* Mildura High School, 1987
Monbulk College	*Monbulk College – Celebrating 50 Years*, Monbulk College, 2013
Moorleigh High School	Gray, Moira, *A History of Moorleigh High School from 1966 to 1986*, Moorleigh High School, 1986
Morwell High School	Maddern, I.T. (Ivan Theodore), *History of Morwell High School*, Vols. 1–7, Morwell High School, n.d. 1966–1967?

Morwell Technical School	Sutton, Ellen E. (Compiler), *A History of Morwell Technical School 1959–1986*, Morwell Technical School, 1986
Mount Waverley High School	*Unicorn Comes of Age: Mount Waverley High School Celebrates its 21st Year, 1964–1984*, Mount Waverley High School, 1984
Murrayville High School	Millikin, Marie, *From Mallee Scrub to a Secondary College, 1969–1989: Looking Towards the Future for Our Children*, Murrayville High School Reunion Committee, 1989
Murtoa College I	*Murtoa Secondary College 1924–1994 Reunion School History Booklet*, Murtoa Secondary College, 1994 *Murtoa 1549 125 years of Primary Education*, Murtoa Primary School, 2000 *Murtoa School No. 1549 1875–1975*, Murtoa Primary School, 1975
Nathalia Secondary College	Oakes, Marion I., *History of Nathalia Higher Elementary School 1919–1958 and Nathalia High School 1959–1985*, Nathalia High School, 1985 Loger, Lyn, Oakes, Marion I., *Memories and History of Nathalia Secondary College: 1990–2009: Including Nathalia High School 1959–1989 and Nathalia Higher Elementary School 1919–1958*, Nathalia Secondary College, c.2009
Neerim & District Secondary College	Rochford, John T. *A School of Our Own – A History of Secondary Schooling in the Neerim District*, Neerim & District Secondary College, 2003

Newlands High Schol	Tabbernee, W., *A history of Newlands High School, 1959 to 1968*, Newlands High School, 1968
Norlane High School	Billett, Janet (ed.), *Onward and Upward: The History of Norlane High School, 1958–1988*, Norlane High School, 1982 *Norlane Remembers, 1957–2007*, DVD, Norlane High School, 2007
Northcote High School	Israel, Gary, Bereson, Itiel, Bridges, Robert and Gallagher, Hector, *The Green, the Purple and the Gold: A History of Northcote High School*, Northcote High School, 2010
Orbost Secondary College	*Orbost High School 1912–1987: 75 Years*, Orbost High School, 1987 Phillips, John, *A Century of Secondary Education at Orbost 1912–2012*, Orbost Secondary College, 2012
Ouyen High School	Back to Ouyen High School Committee, *Ouyen High School 1929–1979* *Tales and Times of Ouyten Primary School 1909–1989*, Sunnyland Press, Red Cliffs, 1989
Pascoe Vale Girls' College	Atkinson, Julie, Eunson, Cynthia, Griffin, Cheryl (Compilers), *Memories of Pascoe Vale Girls College: 1956–2006*, Pascoe Vale Girls' College, 2006
Portland Technical School	McDougall, Brenda (Compiler), *Portland Technical School: The First Twenty Years*, Becombe Printers, 1990

Prahran Technical School	*Jubilee: Prahran Technical School 1915–1965*, Prahran Technical School, 1965 Buckrick, Judith Raphael, *Design for Living: A History of 'Prahran Tech'*, Prahran Mechanics' Institute Press, 2007
Preston East Technical School	*Glimpses of the Past: A Brief History of Preston East Technical School,* Preston East Technical School, 1985
Preston Girls' High School	Sharpe, Barbara, *Greylings 1928–1978*, Preston Girls' High School, 1977 Sharpe, Barbara (ed.), *The Life and Times of a Preston Girl: An Eye-Opening Wander Through 75 – Plus Years of a School and Its Society,* Preston Girls Secondary College, New Generation Print and Copy, 2004
Princes Hill High School	Vlahogiannis, Nicholas, *Prinny Hill: The State Schools of Princes Hill, 1889–1989,* 1989
Pyramid Hill College	Stevens, Helen, *From Slate to Computer: A History of Pyramid Hill and District Schools*, Espress Printer, 2005
Rainbow High School	Rainbow High School (Form 5 History Class), *Schooldays North of the Vermin Proof Fence*, Rainbow High School, 1978
Red Cliffs High School	*Making Good Better: A History of Red Cliffs High School,* Sunnyland Press, 1985
Reservoir High School	*Fifty Years of Secondary Education at Plenty Road Reservoir 1950–2004,* Graphics Unlimited, 2004 *Reservoir High School 1954–1979: A History to Celebrate the Silver Jubilee of Reservoir High School,* Reservoir High School, 1979

Ringwood Secondary College	Heritage Group, *Ringwood Recalls: The First Fifty Years of Ringwood High School/Ringwood Secondary College 1954–2004*, Heritage Group, 2004
Rushworth High School	*Twenty-Five Years at Rushworth High School 1961–1985*, pamphlet, Rushworth High School, 1985
Sale High School	Synan, Ann & Peter, *Sale High School Centenary Memories*, Sale College, 2007 Synan, T.P., *From Plough to Computer: The Story of the Sale High School*, Gippsland Times, n.d.
Sale Technical School	Lewis, Pamela *The Centenary History of Sale Technical School*, Sale Technical School, 1985
Sandringham High School	Joy, Shirley M. *Education in Sandringham, Victoria, Australia: Glimpses into the Past – Commencing 1897*, Shirley M. Joy, 2006
Seaford-Carrum High School	*Seaford-Carrum High School, 25th Anniversary 1967–1991*, pamphlet, Seaford-Carrum High School, 1991
Shepparton High School	Martindale, H.G., *The Story of the Shepparton High School*, Advisory Council, 1946 Michael, Ron, *From Mr Chips to Micro-Chips: The High School, Shepparton, 1909–1984*, Waterwheel Press, 1984 Waldron, Lorraine, *Index to the Story of the Shepparton High School by H.G. Martindale*, published by the authority of the Advisory Council, 1946, Shepparton Family History Group, 2009 Kilfoyle, Helena, McLean, Rae, *A Century Not Out 1909–2009: Shepparton High School*, Shepparton High School, 2009

Shepparton Technical College	Vibert, V.E., *Shepparton Technical College, 1953–1978, Silver Jubilee*, Biggs Printing Service, 1978
Springvale High School	Blaze, B.R., *The Springtime of Springvale High: A Chronicle of the Earliest Years of Springvale High School, Victoria*, Springvale High School?, 1978? Cunningham, Margaret, *Springvale High School, 1954–1994: A Multicultural Tradition*, Springvale High School?, 1994?
St Arnaud High School	Healey, Vern, *St Arnaud High School: 75 Years, 1914–1989*, Creative Rural Printers, 1989
St Helena Secondary College	*St Helena Secondary College: St Helena Post Primary School, 1983–1998: Foundation Years from Planning to Reality*, St Helena Secondary College, 1999?
Sunshine Technical School	*Sunshine Technical School 1913–1991: A Scrap Book*, Sunshine Technical School, 1991
Swan Hill High School	Gardner, Graeme, Braybrook, Phyl, *Yours and My School: Swan Hill High School, 1928–1990*, Swan Hill High School, 1990
Swift's Creek School	*Swifts' Creek School 1460, Centenary 1874–1974*, Swift's Creek School, 1974 *125 Years Between the Gap: A Celebration of Education: The Histories of Fifteen Schools Are Commemorated in This Book, an exciting Journey from Rough Log Shanties to Star Lab*, Swift's Creek Primary School, 1999
Tottenham Community Secondary College	Harewood, Jocelyn, *The History of Tottenham Technical School, 1957–1991: An Era Gone By*, Tottenham Community Secondary College, 1991

Tyntynder Central School	Durden, Shirley, *Tyntynder Central School & District: 80 Years*, Tyntynder Central Back-to Committee, 1993
University High School	Hoy, Alice, *A City Built to Music: The History of University High School, Melbourne, 1910 to 1960*, University High School, 1961 (R) White, Yvette (ed.), *A Record of the Sixties and Seventies*, University High School, Parkville, 1985 (R) Rasmussen, Carolyn, *A Whole New World: 100 Years of Education at University High School*, Melbourne, Australian Scholarly Publishing, 2010
Upper Yarra Secondary College	Baddeley, Peter J., *Learning Through the Seasons: The History of Upper Yarra Secondary College, 1961–1994*, Upper Yarra Secondary College, 1994
Upwey High School	Myers, Richard, *First in the Hills: Upwey High School, 1937–1987*, Upwey High School, c.1987
Victorian School for Deaf Children	Burchett, J. H., *Utmost for the Highest: The Story of the Victorian School for Deaf Children*, Halls Book Store Pty. Ltd., 1964
Wallara	*Celebrating a 50 Year Journey 1959–2009*, Wallara, 1959
Wangaratta High School	Healey, Meredith, Barr Lynton, Barr, Dawn & Humphry, Rose, *History of Wangaratta High School 1909–1984, Researched by Year 11 1983 History Class*, Wangaratta High School, 1984 Jones, Graham, *Wangaratta High School, 90 years on, 1909–1999*, Charquin Hill, 1999 Gallagher, Trish, *Celebrate!: The First 100 Years of Wangaratta High School, 1909–2009*, Wangaratta High School, 2009

Wantirna College	Gavin, Paul (ed.), *Wantirna High School: A 20-Year Success Story: 1980–2000*, Wantirna College, 2000
Warragul High School	*Warragul High School, 75th Anniversary, 1911–1986: A Review*, Warragul High School, 1986
Warragul Regional College	Haughton, Jenny, *The School on the Hill 1911–2011: Celebrating 100 Years of State Secondary Education in Warragul*, Warragul Regional College Council, 2011
Warrnambool High School	Hando, Regina, *The School on the Hill: Reminiscences on the 75th Anniversary of Warrnambool High School*, Warrnambool High School, 1982
Warrnambool College	Welsford, Ray, *100 Years of Service: A Centenary History of Warrnambool College*, Star Printing Service, 2007
Wellington Secondary College	*Transition Change and Continuity in Wellington Secondary College 1998–2002*, Wellington Secondary College, 2002 (R) *In the Wellington Way*, Wellington Secondary College, 1997
Westall High School	Zigouras, Vernita, *Westall High School: A History 1963 to 1988*, Westall High School, 1988
White Hills Technical School	Thomas, Ken, *White Hills Technical School: The First Thirty Years 1961–1990*, White Hills Secondary College, 1991?

Williamstown High School	Williamstown High School Ex-Students & Staff Association Inc., *Williamstown High School Pictorial: A Walk Through Some of Williamstown High School's Collection of Photos for Ex-Students and Students*, Williamstown High School Ex-Students and Staff Association, 2005? *Williamstown High School Anecdotes: A Collection of Anecdotes from Ex-Students and Staff*, 2 vols., Book One: Williamstown High School, 2007, Book Two: Williamstown High School, 2008
Winchelsea Higher Elementary School	Gladman, Ian, *Winchelsea Higher Elementary School: Centenary, 1878–1978*, Ken Jenkins Print, 1978
Wodonga High School	50 Years of Wodonga High School: 1954–2004, Wodonga High School, 2004
Wonthaggi Technical School	*Wonthaggi Technical School, golden jubilee 1972*, Wonthaggi Technical School, 1972

Websites

Many schools have also provided histories, ranging from the brief to the expansive and detailed on their websites. Web addresses were accurate as at 17 March 2015.

School	History
Alvie CoS	http://www.alvie-cs.vic.edu.au/index.php?option=com_content&view=article&id=7&Itemid=7
Ararat College	http://www.araratcc.vic.edu.au/page14.html
Baden Powell P-9 College, Tarneit	http://www.bpc.vic.edu.au/index.php?option=com_content&view=article&id=57&Itemid=61
Ballarat SC	http://www.ballaratsc.vic.edu.au/
Balmoral K-12 Community College	http://www.balmoralcommunitycollege.vic.edu.au/about-bcc/history/
Bendigo Senior SC	https://www.bssc.edu.au/college/history
Bendigo SDS	http://www.bendigosds.vic.edu.au/page/60/School-History
Blackwood Special Schools Outdoor Education Centre	http://www.blackwoodssoec.vic.edu.au/03_our_orgainsation/webpage_05_history/history.html

Bogong Outdoor Education Centre	http://www.boec.vic.edu.au/our-school/#history
Boronia Heights K-12 College	http://www.boroniak-12.vic.edu.au/our-college/history/
Brauer College, Warrnambool	http://www.brauer.vic.edu.au/index.php?option=com_content&view=article&id=7&Itemid=121
Braybrook College	http://www braybrooksc.vic.edu.au/about-2/history
Bright P-12 College	http://www.brightp12.vic.edu.au/
Brighton SC	http://www.brightonsc.vic.edu.au/pages.aspx?pageURL=bschistory
Camperdown College	http://www.camperdowncoll.vic.edu.au/app/webroot/uploaded_files/media/school_history.pdf
Canterbury Girls' SC	http://www.cgsc.vic.edu.au/our-school/history
Chaffey SC, Mildura	http://www.chaffeysc.vic.edu.au/html/about/history.html
Coburg High School	http://www.pandora.nla.gov.au/tep/119845
Cohuna SC	http://www.cohuna-sc.vic.edu.au/pages/our-story.html
Colac SC	http://www.colac-sc.vic.edu.au
Colac SpS	http://www.colacspecialistschool.vic.edu.au

Collingwood College	http://www.collingwood.vic.edu.au/about-us/history/
Corryong College	http://www.corryong.vic.edu.au/about/history
Daylesford SC	http://www.daylesfordsc.vic.edu.au/history/
Derrinallum P-12 College	http://www.derrinallump12.vic.edu.au/school-history.html
Dimboola Memorial SC	http://www.dmsc.vic.edu.au/about_us/history.html
Dromana SC	http://www.dsc.vic.edu.au/index.php/our-college/history-tradition
Drouin SC	http://www.student.drouinsc.vic.edu.au/wordpress/history/
Dunkeld CoS	http://www.dunkeld.vic.edu.au/page/54/School-History
Elisabeth Murdoch College	http://www.emc.vic.edu.au/about-elisabeth-murdoch-college/history.html
Eltham HS	http://www.elthamhs.vic.edu.au/history.html
Essendon – Keilor College	http://www.ekc.vic.edu.au/category/campus/our-college/history
Euroa SC	http://www.euroasc.vic.edu.au/?page_id=374
Furlong Park School for Deaf Children, Sunshine North	http://www.furlongpark.vic.edu.au/About_history.html
Geelong HS	http://www.geelonghigh.vic.edu.au/about-history

Gilmore College for Girls, Footscray	http://www.gilmoregirls.vic.edu.au/RichInHistory
Hallam Senior College	http://www.hallamssc.vic.edu.au/en-AU/content/college-history
Hume Central SC	http://www.humecentralsc.vic.edu.au/aboutus/school-history-and-council.html
Joseph Banks SC, Doveton	http://www.hostftpservers.com/2097/doveton
Kaniva P-12 College	http://www.kanivacollege.vic.edu.au/history.htm
Katandra School, Ormond	http://www.katandra.vic.edu.au/history-katandra-school
Kensington Community HS	http://www.kchs.vic.edu.au/cms-about-us/history-of-the-school.phps
Kew HS	http://www.kew.vic.edu.au/articles/29
Koo Wee Rup SC	http://www.kwrsc.vic.edu.au/about/our-history/
Kyneton SC	http://www.kynsec.vic.edu.au/about.html
Lakes Entrance SC	http://www.lakessc.vic.edu.au/history.html
Lalor SC	http://www.lalorsc.vic.edu.au/history-of-lsc
Leongatha SC	http://www.leonsec.vic.edu.au/about_history.html
MacRobertson GHS	http://www.macrob.vic.edu.au/our_history
Macleod College	http://www.macleod.vic.edu.au/pages/history.html

Melbourne HS	http://www.mhsviceduau.com/#!history/c1eiy
Mentone Girls' SC	http://www.mgsc.vic.edu.au/our-college/history
Mildura Senior College	http://www.milsen.vic.edu.au/?page_id=204
Montague CEC	http://www.montague.vic.edu.au/page/55/School-History
Mont Albert CS	http://www.maps.vic.edu.au/page/57/School-History
Mount Alexander SC	http://www.mountalexandercollege.vic.edu.au/about/history/
Mount Eliza SC	http://www.mesc.vic.edu.au/?page_id=2760
Naranga School, Frankston	http://www.naranga.vic.edu.au/?page_id=124
Northcote HS	http://www.nhs.vic.edu.au/index.php?q=about-us/heritage
Nossal HS	http://www.nossalhs.vic.edu.au/about-nossal/history
Pakenham SC	http://www.pakenhamsc.vic.edu.au/history.html
Portland SC	http://www.portlandsc.vic.edu.au/our-school/our-history
Red Cliffs Secondary College	http://www.red-cliffs-sc.vic.edu.au/our_history.html
Ringwood SC	http://www.ringwoodsc.vic.edu.au/heritage

Sandringham College	http://www.sandringhamsc.vic.edu.au/our-college/history/
Shepparton HS	http://www2.shs.vic.edu.au/about-us/history.html
Sherbroke Community School	http://www.sherbrooke.vic.edu.au/history.html
Staughton College, Melton	http://www.staughtoncollege.vic.edu.au/Latest/School-History/
Strathmore SC	http://www.strathmore.vic.edu.au/about/about_history.aspx
Sunshine College	http://www.sunshine.vic.edu.au/history.htm
The Lakes South Morang P-9 School	http://www.thelakes.edu.au/index.php?page=our-history
Thornbury HS	http://www.thornburyhs.vic.edu.au/about/history-of-school
Timboon P-12 School	http://www.timboonp12.vic.edu.au/page/174/School-History
University HS	http://www.unihigh.vic.edu.au/index.php?option=com_content&view=article&id=13&Itemid=18
Victorian College for the Deaf, St Kilda Road	http://www.vcd.vic.edu.au/wordpress/?page_id=56
Victorian College of The Arts Secondary School	http://www.vcass.vic.edu.au/about/history/

Victorian School of Languages	http://www.vsl.vic.edu.au/AboutUs.php
Viewbank College	http://www.viewbank.vic.edu.au/our-history
Warragul Regional College	http://www.wrc.vic.edu.au/about-wrc/history/
Warrandyte HS	http://www.warrandytehigh.vic.edu.au/history.html
Weeroona College Bendigo	http://www.weeroona.vic.edu.au/?page_id=196
Whittlesea SC	http://www.whittleseasc.vic.edu.au/history-whittlesea-secondary-college
Williamstown HS	http://www.willihigh.vic.edu.au/?page_id=78
Yea HS	http://www.yeahs.vic.edu.au/Our-School/Our-History/

About the Authors

Dr John Andrews, with a PhD in Australian cultural history, taught in government schools across Melbourne. As well he worked in teacher education and curriculum development, particularly on Australia's Bicentenary education program, the Studies of Society and Environment Course Advice Project, in civics and citizenship, history, environmental education and Victoria's Centenary of Federation education program. Following 37 years with the Education Department, John has developed numerous curriculum materials for commercial publishers, museums and historical sites, receiving the 2008 AGTA award and sharing the 2010 Medium Museums Award for the Shrine's Outreach Program.

Social scientist, historian and author, **Dr Deborah Towns** taught in government schools and the tertiary education sector and has held leadership roles in community, public and private organisations. Her PhD, '"Their Own Sphere" Women Teachers in the Education Department of Victoria 1880s–1980s' provided her with the opportunity to build upon her knowledge of equity and diversity in education and employment. A researcher in the Centre for Workplace Leadership, Faculty of Business and Economics, University of Melbourne, she has recent publications in leadership, human resource management, women's history and education.

www.ingramcontent.com/pod-product-compliance
Ingram Content Group Australia Pty Ltd
76 Discovery Rd, Dandenong South VIC 3175, AU
AUHW020134130726
429791AU00003B/134

9 781925 588507